STUDENT UNIT GUIDE

CCEA AS Chemistry Unit 1

Basic Concepts in Physical and Inorganic Chemistry

Alyn G. McFarland

Philip Allan, an imprint of Hodder Education, an Hachette UK company, Market Place, Deddington, Oxfordshire OX15 0SE

Orders
Bookpoint Ltd, 130 Milton Park, Abingdon, Oxfordshire OX14 4SB
tel: 01235 827827
fax: 01235 400401
e-mail: education@bookpoint.co.uk
Lines are open 9.00 a.m.–5.00 p.m., Monday to Saturday, with a 24-hour message answering service.
You can also order through the Philip Allan website: www.philipallan.co.uk

ISBN 978-1-4441-7855-5

First printed 2012
Impression number 5 4
Year 2017 2016 2015

Cover photo: Fotolia

Typeset by Integra Software Services Pvt. Ltd., Pondicherry, India

Printed in India

Hachette UK's policy is to use papers that are natural, renewable and recyclable products and made from wood grown in sustainable forests. The logging and manufacturing processes are expected to conform to the environmental regulations of the country of origin.

Contents

Getting the most from this book

Examiner tips

Advice from the examiner on key points in the text to help you learn and recall unit content, avoid pitfalls, and polish your exam technique in order to boost your grade.

Knowledge check

Rapid-fire questions throughout the Content Guidance section to check your understanding.

Knowledge check answers

1 Turn to the back of the book for the Knowledge check answers.

Summary

Summaries

- Each core topic is rounded off by a bullet-list summary for quick-check reference of what you need to know.

Questions & Answers

Exam-style questions

Examiner comments on the questions
Tips on what you need to do to gain full marks, indicated by the icon ⓔ.

Sample student answers
Practise the questions, then look at the student answers that follow each set of questions.

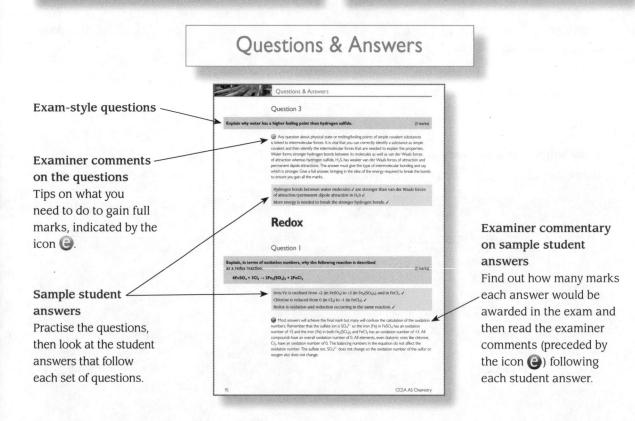

Examiner commentary on sample student answers
Find out how many marks each answer would be awarded in the exam and then read the examiner comments (preceded by the icon ⓔ) following each student answer.

About this book

This book will guide you through CCEA AS Chemistry Unit 1: Basic Concepts in Physical and Inorganic Chemistry. It has two sections:

- The **Content Guidance** section covers all of Unit 1 and includes helpful examiner tips on how to approach revision and improve exam technique. Do not skim over these tips as they provide important guidance. There are also Knowledge check questions throughout this section, with answers at the end of the book. At the end of each section there is a summary of the key points covered. There are several areas in this unit that are essential to other units in the course — for example, atomic structure, bonding, shapes of molecules, intermolecular forces and redox. These topics and indeed all the content of this unit can be examined synoptically in A2 units.
- The **Questions and Answers** section gives sample examination questions on each topic as well as worked answers and examiner comments on the common pitfalls to avoid. The examination will consist of 10 multiple-choice questions (each with four options, A to D), followed by several structured questions. This Question and Answer section contains many different examples of questions, but you should also refer to past papers for this unit, which are available online.

Both the Content Guidance and Questions and Answers sections are divided into the topics outlined by the CCEA specification.

General tips

- Be accurate with your learning at this level as examiners will penalise incorrect wording.
- For any calculation, always follow it through to the end even if you feel you have made a mistake, as there are marks for the correct method even if the final answer is incorrect.
- Always attempt to answer a multiple-choice question even if it is a guess (you have a 25% chance of getting it right).
- When answering a question involving a colour of a chemical you must be accurate to obtain the marks. If a colour of a chemical is given in this book with a hyphen (-) between the colours then state the two colours exactly like that including the hyphen, e.g. bromine is red-brown so both red and brown are required separated by a hyphen. If two or more colours are given separated by a forward slash (/), these are alternative answers and only **one** colour from this list should be given, e.g. for the yellow/orange flame test for Na$^+$ ions, only yellow on its own or orange on its own will be accepted but **not** a combination of the two colours. Never use a forward slash (/) when answering a colour question. If only one colour is given for a chemical then use this single colour, e.g. white for the colour of the precipitate when silver nitrate solution is added to a solution containing chloride ions. This applies to all CCEA AS and A2 examinations. Check the colour document on the CCEA chemistry microsite (www.ccea.org.uk/chemistry) then select revised GCE for further guidance should this change.

The uniform mark you receive for each of Unit 1 and Unit 2 will be out of 105. Unit 3 (examining practical work and planning from AS1 and AS2) is awarded out of 90 uniform marks, giving a possible total of 300 for AS Chemistry.

Content Guidance

Formulae, equations and amounts of substance

Type of formulae

There are two main types of chemical formula: empirical and molecular. An **empirical formula** shows the simplest ratio of the atoms of each element. This type of formula is used for ionic compounds and macromolecules (giant covalent molecules). Examples include NaCl (ionic), MgO (ionic), $CaCl_2$ (ionic) and SiO_2 (macromolecular).

A **molecular formula** shows the actual number of atoms of each element in one molecule of the substance. This is used for all molecular (simple) covalent substances. Examples include H_2O, CO_2, O_2, CH_4, NH_3, H_2O_2, I_2 and S_8 (all molecular covalent).

Some elements exist as simple molecules. These are the diatomic elements (H_2, N_2, O_2, F_2, Cl_2, Br_2, I_2), sulfur (S_8) and phosphorus (P_4).

Writing chemical formulae

Valency is the combining power of an atom or an ion. For all compounds the valency must be determined for each atom or ion in the compound and this is then used to write the formula of the compound.

Determining valency of atoms

Valency can be determined from the group in which the element is found in the Periodic Table (Table 1).

Table 1 Group numbers and common valencies

Group number	Most common valency
I	1
II	2
III	3
IV	4
V	3
VI	2
VII	1
VIII	—

The atoms of Group VIII elements do not generally form compounds so they have no common valency. Hydrogen always has a valency of 1. Transition metals have variable valency, the most common being 2. The valency of a transition metal atom is usually given by a roman numeral in brackets after the name, for example iron(III) chloride — iron has a valency of 3 in this compound. If no roman numeral is given then assume the valency is 2, except for silver, which has a valency of 1.

The valency of a Group I atom is always 1 and for a Group II atom it is always 2.

The valencies of the atoms of elements in Groups III to VII do vary and again they can be given as a roman numeral after the name of the element. For example: in nitrogen(I) oxide, nitrogen has a valency of 1; in sulfur(VI) oxide, sulfur has a valency of 6.

Many compounds have common names, which are often used, such as water, ammonia, methane, carbon dioxide, sulfur trioxide and carbon monoxide. Some of these names give a clue to the formula, for example carbon dioxide — dioxide means there are two oxygen atoms in the compound. For some others the formulae of the compounds will have to be learned.

Determining valency of ions

- The valency of an ion is simply the same as the size of the charge on the ion. Remember that metal ions are positive; as a general rule, non-metal ions are negative.
- The charge on a simple ion of elements in groups I, II and III (except boron, which does not form a positive ion) is positive and has the magnitude of the Group number. For example:
  - K is in Group I so its simple ion is K^+; valency = 1
  - Mg is in Group II so its simple ion is Mg^{2+}; valency = 2
  - Al is in Group III so its simple ion is Al^{3+}; valency = 3
- The charge on a simple ion of elements in Groups V, VI, and VII is negative and has the magnitude of 8 minus the group number. For example:
  - N is in Group V so its simple ion is N^{3-} (8 − 5 = 3); valency = 3
  - O is in Group VI so its simple ion is O^{2-} (8 − 6 = 2); valency = 2
  - F is in Group VII so its simple ion is F^- (8 − 7 = 1); valency = 1
- Non-metals in Group IV (C and Si) do not form common simple ions.
- Metals in Group IV form common 2+ ions, for example Pb^{2+} and Sn^{2+}.
- Hydrogen forms a positive hydrogen ion (H^+) and a negative hydride ion (H^-).
- Transition elements have variable valency and form a variety of simple ions. For example:
  - iron(III) has a valency of 3 and the ion is Fe^{3+}
  - copper(II) has a valency of 2 and the ion is Cu^{2+}
  - silver(I) has a valency of 1 and the ion is Ag^+
- Iron(III) ions are Fe^{3+}; copper(II) ions are Cu^{2+}; sodium ions are Na^+.
- Oxide ions are O^{2-}; chloride ions are Cl^-; nitride ions are N^{3-}.
- Molecular ions are charged particles made up of more than one atom. Common examples are shown in Table 2. The valency of a molecular ion is the same as the size of the charge, for example sulfate is SO_4^{2-}, so a single sulfate is SO_4 and it has a valency of 2.

Examiner tip
You need to learn the formulae (including charges) of common molecular ions as these are not given to you in the exams as they would have been at GCSE level.

Table 2 Examples of molecular ions

Ion	Formula	Ion	Formula
Sulfate	SO_4^{2-}	Carbonate	CO_3^{2-}
Nitrate	NO_3^-	Hydrogencarbonate	HCO_3^-
Nitrite	NO_2^-	Sulfite	SO_3^{2-}
Hydrogensulfate	HSO_4^-	Hypochlorite	OCl^-
Dichromate(VI)	$Cr_2O_7^{2-}$	Manganate(VII)	MnO_4^-

Writing formulae using valencies

The scheme shown in Table 3 will allow you to work out the formula of any compound.

Table 3 Using valencies to work out the formula for potassium chloride

	potassium	chloride
(1) Compound name	potassium	chloride
(2) Convert to symbols (or formula if molecular ion)	K	Cl
(3) Group numbers (skip this for molecular ions and transition elements)	I	VII
(4) Valency	I (as Group I)	I (as Group VII)
(5) Write valencies above symbols	$\overset{I}{K}$	$\overset{I}{Cl}$
(6) Cancel down if necessary	–	–
(7) Cross over the valency values	$\overset{I}{K}$	$\overset{I}{Cl}$
(8) Write together with crossed-over valencies as subscripts (use brackets if a molecular ion is multiplied by 2 or more)	K_1Cl_1	
(9) Ignore 1s (as $K_1 = K$)	KCl	

Examiner tip
There is no need to cancel the valencies in this example but if the valencies of both elements were 2, these would cancel down to 1 and 1 before cross over.

Tables 4–7 apply this technique to other formulae.

Table 4

Calcium oxide	Ca	O
Group numbers	II	VI
Valency	2	2
	$\overset{2}{Ca}$	$\overset{2}{O}$
	$\overset{1}{Ca}$	$\overset{1}{O}$
	CaO	

Table 5

Aluminium oxide	Al	O
Group numbers	III	VI
Valency	3	2
	$\overset{3}{Al}$	$\overset{2}{O}$
	Al_2O_3	

Table 6

Iron(III) chloride	Fe	Cl
Group numbers	–	VII
Valency	3	I
	$\overset{3}{Fe}$	$\overset{I}{Cl}$
	$FeCl_3$	

Table 7

Calcium hydroxide	Ca	OH
Group numbers	II	–
Valency	2	I
	$\overset{2}{Ca}$	$\overset{I}{OH}$
	$Ca(OH)_2$	

Formulae of ionic compounds from the ions

The formula of an ionic compound can be determined simply from the charges on the ions, as the overall charge on an ionic compound must be zero.

- Sodium chloride contains Na^+ and Cl^- ions.
  1 of each ion is required, so sodium chloride is NaCl.

Remember that chemical formulae are written without the charges.

- Calcium chloride contains Ca^{2+} and Cl^- ions.
  2 Cl^- ions are required for 1 Ca^{2+} ion, so calcium chloride is $CaCl_2$.
- Magnesium oxide contains Mg^{2+} and O^{2-} ions.
  1 of each ion is required, so magnesium oxide is MgO.
- Copper(II) hydroxide contains Cu^{2+} and OH^- ions.
  2 OH^- ions are required for 1 Cu^{2+} ion, so calcium hydroxide is $Cu(OH)_2$.
- Ammonium sulfate contains NH_4^+ and SO_4^{2-} ions.
  2 NH_4^+ ions are required for 1 SO_4^{2-} ion, so ammonium sulfate is $(NH_4)_2SO_4$.
- Aluminium nitrate contains Al^{3+} and NO_3^- ions.
  3 NO_3^- ions are required for 1 Al^{3+} ion, so aluminium nitrate is $Al(NO_3)_3$.

Examiner tip

The hydroxide ion is a unit and so when we have more than one of them we must use brackets. This is true of all molecular ions.

Examiner tip

Errors with formulae often involve: hydroxides of metals with valency greater than I; carbonates and sulfates of metals with valency I; or ammonium carbonate and sulfate:

- Often brackets are left out, e.g. calcium hydroxide is often *incorrectly* written as $CaOH_2$ instead of $Ca(OH)_2$.
- The two metal or ammonium ions may not be included in the formula, e.g. potassium sulfate is often *incorrectly* written as KSO_4 instead of K_2SO_4.
- Examples of *correct* sulfate and carbonate formulae are: Na_2CO_3, Na_2SO_4, K_2CO_3, $(NH_4)_2SO_4$.

Balanced symbol equations

A balanced symbol equation shows the rearrangement of atoms in a chemical reaction.

Worked example 1

Magnesium reacts with oxygen according to the word equation:

magnesium + oxygen → magnesium oxide

To convert this to a balanced symbol equation, write the correct formulae of all the substances present as shown in Figure 1.

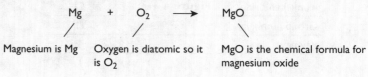

Magnesium is Mg   Oxygen is diatomic so it is O_2 MgO is the chemical formula for magnesium oxide

Figure 1

> **Examiner tip**
> Remember you cannot change a formula to balance an equation (Figure 2).

However, the equation is not balanced as there are 2 oxygen atoms on the left-hand side and only one oxygen atom on the right-hand side. To balance the equation you can put balancing numbers in front of a formula, e.g. a 2 in front of MgO means that there are now 2 magnesium oxide units, i.e. 2 Mg atoms and 2 O atoms.

Step 1: a 2 here balances the oxygen but creates another issue — there are 2 Mg on the right-hand side, so this now has to be balanced as well

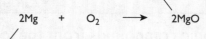

Step 2: with the oxygen now balanced, you need a 2 here in front of the Mg to give 2 Mg atoms and balance the equation

Figure 2

The equation is now balanced; often you have to balance one element which may create another issue with another element.

Worked example 2

Ethane burns completely in air to form carbon dioxide and water (Figure 3).

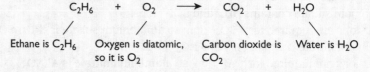

Ethane is C_2H_6 Oxygen is diatomic, so it is O_2 Carbon dioxide is CO_2 Water is H_2O

Figure 3

This equation is not balanced as there are 2 carbon atoms on the left (in C_2H_6) and only 1 carbon atom on the right (in CO_2). Also there are 6 H atoms on the left (in C_2H_6)

and only 2 H atoms on the right (in H_2O), and 2 O atoms on the left (in O_2) but 3 O atoms on the right (2 O in CO_2 and 1 O in H_2O).

Sort out the carbon first (Figure 4).

Step 1: a 2 here balances the carbon atoms

Step 2: a 3 here balances the hydrogen atoms

$$C_2H_6 \;+\; 3\tfrac{1}{2}O_2 \;\longrightarrow\; 2CO_2 \;+\; 3H_2O$$

Step 3: a 3½ here balances the oxygen

Figure 4

> **Examiner tip**
>
> It may seem unusual to balance an equation using fractions. The balancing numbers in the equation can be doubled to avoid the fraction, giving:
>
> $$2C_2H_6 + 7O_2 \rightarrow 4CO_2 + 6H_2O$$
>
> *But* at this level it is fine to use fractions to balance equations, particularly combustion equations.

The mole and Avogadro's number

A balanced symbol equation for a reaction gives the rearrangement of the atoms within a chemical reaction.

Take the equation:

$$C + O_2 \rightarrow CO_2$$

We can read this as 1 C atom reacts with 1 O_2 molecule to form 1 CO_2 molecule.

However, the mass of 1 atom of carbon is approximately 2.0×10^{-23} g. This sort of measurement is not possible and so the number of particles measured must be scaled up, but they will still react in the same ratio. For example, 1 million C atoms will react with 1 million oxygen molecules to form 1 million carbon dioxide molecules. However, the mass of 1 million carbon atoms is $1\,000\,000 \times 2.0 \times 10^{-23} = 2 \times 10^{-17}$ g. This is still too small to be measured. We need to multiply by 6.02×10^{23}. This number is called **Avogadro's number**.

1 C atom has a mass of 2×10^{-23} g, so 6.02×10^{23} C atoms have a mass of approximately 12 g.

The 'amount' of a substance is measured in **moles**. Mole is written as mol for unit purposes.

The equation $C + O_2 \rightarrow CO_2$ can be read as 1 mole of carbon atoms reacts with 1 mol of oxygen molecules to form 1 mol of carbon dioxide molecules.

For any substance the mass of one mole is simply the total of the relative atomic masses of all the atoms that make up the substance:

- 1 mol of Mg = 24 g (RAM of Mg = 24)
- 1 mol of O_2 = 32 g (RAM of O = 16)
- 1 mol of H_2O = 18 g (RAM of H = 1; RAM of O = 16)
- 1 mol of $Ca(OH)_2$ = 74 g (RAM of H = 1; RAM of O = 16; RAM of Ca = 40)
- 1 mol of $Fe_2(SO_4)_3$ = 400 g (RAM of O = 16; RAM of S = 32; RAM of Fe = 56)

  NB: there are 2 mol of Fe atoms, 3 mol of S atoms and 12 mol of O atoms in 1 mol of $Fe_2(SO_4)_3$.

Avogadro's number is often defined as the number of atoms in 12.000 g of carbon-12.

The amount of a substance that contains Avogadro's number (6.02×10^{23}) of particles (atoms, molecules or groups of ions) is called a **mole** of the substance.

Often the total of the relative atomic masses in any substance is referred to as the relative formula mass (RFM).

- RFM of H_2O = 18 (no units required)
- RFM of $Fe_2(SO_4)_3$ = 400

The term molar mass is also used, which means the mass of one mole.

- Molar mass of $Ca(OH)_2$ = $74\,gmol^{-1}$
- Molar mass of O_2 = $32\,gmol^{-1}$

The number of moles of a substance can be calculated from the mass using the expression:

$$\text{number of moles} = \frac{\text{mass (g)}}{\text{RFM}}$$

Using Avogadro's number

Sometimes calculations are set that require the calculation of the mass of one atom or molecule, or a comparison between masses of atoms. Or there may be a comparison between the number of particles (atoms or molecules) in a certain mass of substances.

N_A represents Avogadro's number and is equal to 6.02×10^{23}. This value is given on your Periodic Table at GCE so you do not have to remember it, simply know how to use it.

All these calculations rely on the following expressions:

$$\frac{\text{mass (g)}}{\text{RFM}} = \text{number of moles} = \frac{\text{number of particles}}{N_A}$$

Remember that these can be rearranged to give:

$$\text{mass (g)} = \text{RFM} \times \text{moles}$$

and

$$\text{number of particles} = \text{moles} \times N_A$$

Worked example 1

Calculate the mass of 1 atom of Fe.

$$\text{number of moles of Fe for 1 atom} = \frac{1}{6.02 \times 10^{23}} = 1.66 \times 10^{-24}\,\text{mol}$$

$$\text{mass of 1 iron atom} = 1.66 \times 10^{-24} \times 56 = 9.3 \times 10^{-23}\,\text{g}$$

Worked example 2

Calculate the number of oxygen atoms present in 4.4 g of carbon dioxide.

$$\frac{\text{mass (g)}}{\text{RFM}} = \frac{4.4}{44} = 0.1\,\text{mol} \times N_A = 6.02 \times 10^{22}\,\text{molecules of } CO_2$$

Each CO_2 contains 2 O atoms so number of O atoms = $2 \times 6.02 \times 10^{22} = 1.204 \times 10^{23}$ atoms of O.

Percentage composition

From the formula of a compound, we can calculate the percentage by mass of each of the elements within the compound. This can also be applied to water of crystallisation.

The formula we use for percentage composition by mass is:

$$\text{\% composition of element M in a compound} = \frac{\text{number of atoms of M in compound} \times \text{RAM (M)}}{\text{RFM of compound}} \times 100$$

Knowledge check 1

State the number of atoms in 1 mol of argon gas.

Worked example 3

Calculate the percentage compositions of the elements in sodium chloride.

Sodium chloride   NaCl   RFM = 23 + 35.5 = 58.5

Na   Cl

$\% \text{ Na} = \dfrac{23}{58.5} \times 100 = 39.3\%$

$\% \text{ Cl} = \dfrac{35.5}{58.5} \times 100 = 60.7\%$

Worked example 4

Find the percentage water by mass in copper(II) sulfate-5-water.

Copper(II) sulfate-5-water $CuSO_4.5H_2O$

RFM = 64 + 32 + (4 × 16) + 5 × (2 + 16) = 250

Mass of H_2O = 5 × 18 = 90

$\% \text{ H}_2\text{O} = \dfrac{90}{250} \times 100 = 36\%$

Examiner tip

Always check that the percentage compositions of all the constituent elements add up to 100%.

Worked example 5

Calculate the percentage composition by mass of all the elements in $CaCO_3$.

$CaCO_3$ The relative formula mass is 100.

Ca   The relative formula mass is 40

C   The relative formula mass is 12

3 × O   The relative formula mass is 16 × 3 = 48

Hence the percentage compositions can be calculated.

$\% \text{ Ca} = \dfrac{40}{100} \times 100 = 40\%$

$\% \text{ C} = \dfrac{12}{100} \times 100 = 12\%$

$\% \text{ O} = \dfrac{48}{100} \times 100 = 48\%$

Examiner tip

Obviously when only two elements are present, the percentage of the second element can be calculated from the percentage of the first, as they should add up to 100%. However do not trust this, as your first calculation may be wrong. Always work out *all* the percentages you have been asked for in the question in the way shown here.

Worked example 6

Calculate the percentage composition of carbon in ethane and ethene.

Compound	Ethane	Ethene
Formula	C_2H_6	C_2H_4
RFM	30	28
Number of C atoms × RAM	24	24
% C	$\dfrac{24}{30} \times 100 = 80\%$	$\dfrac{24}{28} \times 100 = 86\%$

(This is why ethene burns with a more sooty flame than ethane due to its higher carbon content.)

Using density

Often when liquids are used the volume of a liquid is given rather than a mass. You will be told the density in g/cm³ (or written as g cm⁻³). Density is related to mass and volume in the following expression:

$$\text{density (g cm}^{-3}) = \frac{\text{mass (g)}}{\text{volume (cm}^3)}$$

This expression can be rearranged as follows:

$$\text{mass (g)} = \text{density (g cm}^{-3}) \times \text{volume (cm}^3)$$

$$\text{volume (cm}^3) = \frac{\text{mass (g)}}{\text{density (g cm}^{-3})}$$

Knowledge check 2

Calculate the percentage of carbon in ethanol, C_2H_5OH to two decimal places.

Examiner tip

The triangle below allows you to remember this easily. Cover up the one you want to make the subject of the expression and the other two will be in the right position. For example cover up mass and you have density and volume on the same line so they are multiplied to give mass. Cover up volume and you have mass above density so volume = mass divided by density. *Take care to use the correct volume units.*

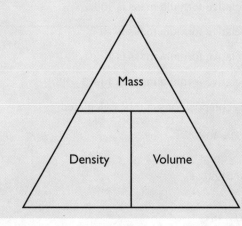

Worked example 7

Calculate the number of moles of mercury in 1 litre given that the density is $13.5\,g\,cm^{-3}$.

Mass (g) = density $(g\,cm^{-3})$ × volume (cm^3)

Mass = 13.5 × 1000 = 13500 g

Number of moles $= \dfrac{13500}{201} = 67.16\,mol$ (RAM of Hg = 201)

Examiner tip

Note that volume has to be in cm^3. 1 litre = 1000 cm^3.

(Remember that 1 ml = 1 cm^3 and 1 dm^3 = 1 litre.)

Finding formulae

The formula of a compound can worked out from the reacting masses, often in the formation of the compound. Or the formula can be determined from the percentage composition by mass.

Worked example 1

Given that 1.06 g of magnesium combines with oxygen to give 1.77 g of magnesium oxide, find the formula of the oxide of magnesium.

Practically this is done by heating a certain mass of magnesium in a crucible with a lid, which is raised periodically to let fresh air in. The magnesium is heated to constant mass to ensure that all the magnesium has combined to form the oxide.
(1) Find the mass of the empty crucible   16.18 g
(2) Find the mass of the crucible and some magnesium   17.24 g
(3) Mass of magnesium = (2) − (1) = 17.24 − 16.18 = 1.06 g
(4) Find the mass of the crucible after heating to constant mass   17.95 g
(5) Mass of oxygen combined = (4) − (2) = 17.95 − 17.24 = 0.71 g

Using the information obtained above we can now calculate the formula of the oxide of magnesium.

Element	Magnesium	Oxygen
Mass (g)	1.06	0.71
RFM	24	16
Moles	$\dfrac{1.06}{24} = 0.044$	$\dfrac{0.71}{16} = 0.044$
Ratio	1	1
Formula = MgO		

As the ratio is 1 Mg atom to 1 O atom, we say that the **empirical formula** is MgO, but it could also be Mg_2O_2 or Mg_3O_3, etc. as the ratio in these compounds is the same.

If the moles work out to be not as simple as the ones shown in Worked example 1, to calculate the ratio, divide all the moles by the smallest number of moles. If you end up with, say, 0.5 then multiply all the ratio numbers by 2 to get whole numbers.

Examiner tip

Always use at least three significant figures when working with numbers less than 1 and three decimal places with numbers greater than 1. This will avoid rounding errors. If a question asks for an exact number of decimal places or significant figures make sure you give a clear answer under these conditions.

The **empirical formula** is the simplest formula that represents the composition by mass of the compound.

Examiner tip

Use 16 for the RFM of oxygen as we are dealing with oxygen atoms combined in the formula.

Worked example 2

4.0 g of hydrated copper(II) sulfate, $CuSO_4.nH_2O$, produces 2.56 g of the anhydrous copper(II) sulfate $CuSO_4$ on heating to constant mass. Find the value of n in the formula of the hydrated salt.

> Mass of hydrated salt = 4.0 g
>
> Mass of anhydrous salt = 2.56 g
>
> Mass of water lost = 4.0 – 2.56 = 1.44 g

Compound	Copper(II) sulfate	Water
Formula	$CuSO_4$	H_2O
Mass (g)	2.56 g	1.44 g
RFM	160	18
Moles	$\dfrac{2.56}{160} = 0.016$	$\dfrac{1.44}{18} = 0.080$
Ratio (÷ 0.0160)	1	5
Empirical formula = $CuSO_4.5H_2O$		

Hence we can see from the empirical formula that the value of $n = 5$.

Worked example 3

An oxide of copper contains 80% copper and 20% oxygen by mass. Find the formula of the compound.

Element	% by mass	RFM	% by mass ÷ RFM (= mole ratio)	Simplest ratio
Copper	80	64	$\dfrac{80}{64} = 1.25$	1
Oxygen	20	16	$\dfrac{20}{16} = 1.25$	1
Empirical formula = CuO				

> **Examiner tip**
>
> If given percentage data, assume you have 100 g and then the percentages become masses, e.g. 80% Cu means 80 g of Cu.

Worked example 4

Hydrated barium chloride contains 56.2% barium, 29.0% chlorine and 14.8% water by mass. Find the formula of the hydrated barium chloride.

Unit	% by mass	RFM	% by mass ÷ RFM (= mole ratio)	Simplest ratio
Barium	56.2	137	$\dfrac{56.2}{137} = 0.41$	1
Chlorine	29.0	35.5	$\dfrac{29.0}{35.5} = 0.82$	2
Water	14.8	18	$\dfrac{14.8}{18} = 0.82$	2
Empirical formula = $BaCl_2.2H_2O$				

Worked example 5

Sodium thiosulfate contains 29.1% sodium, 40.5% chlorine and 30.3% oxygen by mass. Find the formula of the sodium thiosulfate.

Unit	% by mass	RFM	% by mass ÷ RFM (= mole ratio)	Simplest ratio
Sodium	29.1	23	$\dfrac{29.1}{23} = 1.27$	$1 \times 2 = 2$
Sulfur	40.5	32	$\dfrac{40.5}{32} = 1.27$	$1 \times 2 = 2$
Oxygen	30.3	16	$\dfrac{30.3}{16} = 1.89$	$1.5 \times 2 = 3$
Empirical formula = $Na_2S_2O_3$				

Molecular formulae and empirical formulae

The **empirical formula** is the simplest formula that states the composition of the compound. It gives the simplest ratio of all the elements in the compound but the simplest ratio may not be the correct one in terms of the number of each type of atom in a molecule of the compound. For example, ethane has molecular formula C_2H_6 but its empirical formula is CH_3.

The empirical formula mass can be the same as the molar mass. The formula that gives the correct molar mass is the molecular formula. The molecular formula is a multiple of the empirical formula.

> **Knowledge check 3**
>
> What is the empirical formula of $C_6H_4N_2O_4$?

Worked example

The empirical formula of a compound is CH. The molar mass is 78 g/mol. What is the molecular formula of the compound?

Empirical formula = CH

Empirical formula mass = 13 g/mol

Molar mass = 78 g/mol

$$\frac{molar\ mass}{empirical\ formula\ mass} = \frac{78}{13} = 6$$

So,

Molecular formula = 6 × empirical formula

Molecular formula = C_6H_6

Interpreting balanced symbol equations quantitatively

The balanced symbol equation is the key to many mole calculations.

Step 1: Balance the equation correctly using the correct formulae.

Step 2: Using the mass of one of the reactants, which should be given to you, calculate the number of moles of this substance.

Step 3: Using the balancing numbers in the equation, calculate the number of moles of whatever substance you are asked to calculate.

Step 4: Change the number of moles of this substance to mass or volume as required.

Several expressions are required to help you do this:

Expression 1:

$$\text{Number of moles} = \frac{\text{mass (g)}}{\text{RFM}}$$

Expression 2:   Mass (g) = number of moles × RFM

Mass is often written more simply as m. Number of moles is often written as n. Hence the above equations can be learnt in a simplified form as long as you remember what the abbreviations are:

Expression 1:

$$n = \frac{m}{\text{RFM}}$$

Expression 2: $m = n \times \text{RFM}$

Examiner tip

The heating to constant mass in this question refers to that fact that we want all of the 5 g of calcium carbonate to decompose. With the release of carbon dioxide into the atmosphere, the solid will decrease in mass. If we repeatedly heat and check the mass, we will know that all of the calcium carbonate has been decomposed when the mass does not change in successive measurements. This is called heating to constant mass.

Worked example 1

5 g of calcium carbonate is heated to constant mass. What mass of calcium oxide would be obtained?

Step 1: $CaCO_3(s) \rightarrow CaO(s) + CO_2(g)$

Step 2: 5 g of calcium carbonate is the information given. So, using expression 1 this can be converted to moles.

$CaCO_3$ RFM = 100

$$n = \frac{m}{\text{RFM}} = 0.05 \, \text{mol of } CaCO_3$$

Step 3: In the balanced symbol equation given in step 1, there are no balancing numbers so this means that 1 mol of $CaCO_3$ gives 1 mol of CaO and 1 mol of CO_2. So 0.05 mol of $CaCO_3$ gives 0.05 moles of CaO and 0.05 mol of CO_2.

Step 4: To calculate the mass of CaO formed in this reaction, we must use expression 2.

CaO   RFM = 56 $m = n \times \text{RFM}$ $m = 0.05 \times 56 = 2.8 \, \text{g}$

Worked example 2

1.48 g of magnesium nitrate is heated to constant mass. Calculate the mass of magnesium oxide formed in this reaction.

Step 1: $2Mg(NO_3)_2(s) \rightarrow 2MgO(s) + 4NO_2(g) + O_2(g)$

Step 2: 1.48 g of magnesium nitrate is the information given. So, using expression 1 this can be converted to moles:

$Mg(NO_3)_2$ RFM = 148

$$n = \frac{m}{RFM} = \frac{1.48}{148} = 0.01 \, mol$$

Step 3: In the balanced symbol equation given in step 1, there are balancing numbers so this means that 2 mol of $Mg(NO_3)_2$ give 2 mol of MgO, 4 mol of NO_2 and 1 mol of O_2.

So, 0.01 mol of $Mg(NO_3)_2$ gives 0.01 mol of MgO, 0.02 mol of NO_2 and 0.005 mol of O_2.

Step 4: To calculate the mass of MgO formed in this reaction, we must use expression 2.

MgO   RFM = 40 $m = n \times RFM$ $m = 0.01 \times 40 = 0.4 \, g$

> **Knowledge check 4**
>
> Calculate the mass of silver formed when 1.7 g of silver(I) nitrate is heated to constant mass.
>
> $2AgNO_3 \rightarrow 2Ag + O_2 + 2NO_2$

Limiting reactant and excess reactant

Limiting reactant is the reactant in a chemical reaction that limits the amount of product that can be formed. The reaction will stop when all of the limiting reactant is consumed.

Excess reactant is the reactant in a chemical reaction that remains when a reaction stops because the limiting reactant has been completely consumed. The excess reactant remains because there is nothing with which it can react.

Figure 5 shows what happens when complete motorbikes are assembled with an excess of wheels.

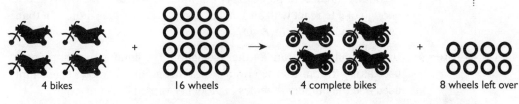

| 4 bikes | 16 wheels | 4 complete bikes | 8 wheels left over |

Figure 5

The bike frames and the wheels on the left represent the reactants. The completed bikes are the product of the reaction. The bike frames are the limiting reactant. The wheels are in excess. This means that the bike frames limit how much product is obtained and there are wheels left over at the end as they are in excess.

Chemically, in the reaction between ammonium chloride and sodium hydroxide 1 mol of ammonium chloride (53.5 g) reacts with 1 mol of sodium hydroxide (40 g):

$$NH_4Cl + NaOH \rightarrow NaCl + NH_3 + H_2O$$

If these exact masses of the reactants are present, then no reactant molecules will be left over at the end of the reaction. However, if 50 g of ammonium chloride are reacted with 40 g of sodium hydroxide, then there is not enough ammonium chloride to react so it is described as the limiting reactant. There is more sodium hydroxide than can react with the ammonium chloride so the sodium hydroxide is in excess (often written as XS).

The limiting reactant and the excess reactant can be determined from the number of moles and using the balanced symbol equation.

Worked example 1

Iron(III) oxide can be reduced using solid carbon according to the equation below:

$$2Fe_2O_3 + 3C \rightarrow 4Fe + 3CO_2$$

16 g of iron(III) oxide were placed in a crucible with 12 g of carbon. The contents were heated until the reaction appeared to be complete. Calculate the mass of iron formed.

Step 1: Calculate number of moles of each substance present initially.

$$\text{Moles of } Fe_2O_3 \text{ used} = \frac{16}{160} = 0.1$$

$$\text{Moles of C used} = \frac{12}{12} = 1$$

(RFM of Fe_2O_3 = 160)   (RFM of C = 12)

Step 2: Using one of the initial moles calculate the number of moles of the other substance required to react using the balanced symbol equation.
Using moles of Fe_2O_3 (either initial moles can be used):

$$2Fe_2O_3 \quad + \quad 3C$$
$$0.1 \qquad\qquad 0.15$$

0.1 mol of Fe_2O_3 requires 0.15 mol of C.

Step 3: Determine which is limiting reactant and which is excess reactant.
1 mol of C is present so Fe_2O_3 is the limiting reactant (as there is not enough of it to react with all 1 mol of C) and C is in XS (as more of it than can react with all of the Fe_2O_3).

Step 4: Use the limiting reactant for the calculation. The limiting reactant is now used as it is the one that determines the other number of moles of reactant used and the number of moles of products formed in the reaction:

$$2Fe_2O_3 + 3C \rightarrow 4Fe + 3CO_2$$
$$0.1 \quad 0.15 \quad 0.2 \quad 0.15$$

0.1 mol of Fe_2O_3 forms 0.2 mol of Fe:

mass of iron formed = 0.2 × 56 = 11.2 g   (RFM of Fe = 56)

Mass of carbon remaining:

mol of carbon left over = 1 − 0.15 (initial mol of C − mol of C reacted)

$$= 0.85 \text{ mol}$$

mass of carbon remaining = 0.85 × 12 = 10.2 g   (RFM of C = 12)

Worked example 2

In the formation of calcium carbide, calcium oxide (quicklime) and carbon (coke) react according to the equation:

$$CaO + 3C \rightarrow CaC_2 + CO$$

What is the maximum mass of calcium carbide that can be obtained from 40 kg of calcium oxide and 40 kg of carbon?

Step 1: Calculate number of moles of each substance present initially.

$$\text{moles of CaO used} = \frac{40000}{56} = 714.29$$

(RFM of CaO = 56; 40 kg = 40 000 g)

$$\text{moles of C used} = \frac{40000}{12} = 3333.33$$

(RFM of C = 12; 40 kg = 40 000 g)

Step 2: Using one of the initial moles calculate the number of moles of the other substance required to react using the balanced symbol equation.
Using moles of CaO (either of the initial moles can be used):

CaO   +   3C

714.29   2142.87

714.29 mol of CaO requires 2142.87 mol of C.

Step 3: Determine which is the limiting reactant and which is the excess reactant.
3333.33 mol of C are present so CaO is the limiting reactant (as there is not enough of it to react with all 3333.33 mol of C) and C is in XS (as more of it than can react with all of the Fe_2O_3).

Step 4: Use the limiting reactant for the calculation. The limiting reactant is now used as it is the one that determines the other number of moles of reactants used and the number of moles of products formed in the reaction.

CaO   +   3C   → CaC_2 +   CO

714.29   2142.87   714.29   714.29

714.29 mol of CaO forms 714.29 mol of CaC_2.
Mass of calcium carbide formed = 714.29 × 64 = 45714.56 g = 45.715 kg
(RFM of CaC_2 = 64)

Water of crystallisation

Many salts (formed from acids) when they are solid are hydrated.

If hydrated salts are heated to constant mass in an open container (so the water vapour can escape) all of the water of crystallisation is removed to leave an anhydrous salt.

A **hydrated** salt contains water of crystallisation. Water of crystallisation comprises water molecules chemically bonded within a crystal structure.

An **anhydrous** salt contains no water of crystallisation.

Figure 6 shows how the hydrated salt may be heated in an evaporating basin. The process of heating to constant mass is often asked about in terms of the steps you would take — you would heat and weigh and repeat this process until the mass no longer changes.

Questions often ask what initial weighings you would make in this type of procedure. You should weigh the empty container and also the mass of the container with the hydrated salt.

Hydrated salts are written with the water of crystallisation — for example, $CuSO_4.5H_2O$, $CoCl_2.6H_2O$ or $Na_2CO_3.10H_2O$.

The number of moles of water of crystallisation attached to 1 mol of the salt is called the degree of hydration. Many hydrated salts effloresce when left in the open. This means they lose their water of crystallisation gradually to the atmosphere. Heating in an open container removes the water of crystallisation more rapidly. Heating a hydrated salt to constant mass will remove all of the water of crystallisation (Figure 6).

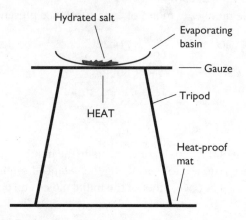

Figure 6 Removing water of crystallisation

The degree of hydration can be determined by taking mass measurements before heating and after heating to constant mass.

Method of calculation

In any question where you are asked to determine the degree of hydration from mass values, follow the flow chart in Figure 7.

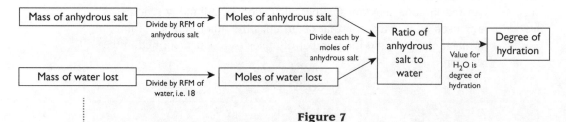

Figure 7

Use the data given to determine the mass of the anhydrous salt and the mass of water lost. From these masses, divide by the RFM and determine the moles of each. The hydrated salt breaks up as shown below:

$$\text{hydrated salt} \rightarrow \text{anhydrous salt} + n\text{H}_2\text{O}$$

$$\text{1 mol} \qquad \text{1 mol} \qquad n\text{ moles}$$

The ratio of the anhydrous salt to the water is 1:n. So convert the moles to a simple ratio in which the anhydrous salt is 1 and the value for water is the degree of hydration.

Worked example

A sample of hydrated sodium carbonate, $Na_2CO_3.xH_2O$ was heated to constant mass in an evaporating basin. The following mass measurements were made.

- Mass of evaporating basin = 53.07 g **(1)**
- Mass of evaporating basin and hydrated sodium carbonate = 58.79 g **(2)**
- Mass of evaporating basin and solid after heating to constant mass = 55.19 g **(3)**

Note the following:
- Mass of anhydrous salt = **(3)** – **(1)**
- Mass of water lost = **(2)** – **(3)**

From the data given, the masses and moles need to be determined (Figure 8).

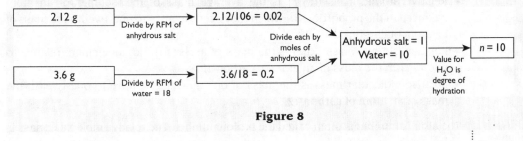

Figure 8

- An empirical formula is the simplest ratio of the atoms in a compound.
- Empirical formulae are used for giant covalent compounds and ionic compounds.
- One mole of a substance is the mass in grams that contains Avogadro's number of particles (6.02×10^{23}).
- A balanced symbol equation is the ratio of the number of moles of each reactant and product.

- In a chemical reaction one or more reactants is often in excess and there will be one reactant, described as the limiting reactant, which limits the number of moles of product formed based on this number of moles of reactant.
- Heating a hydrated compound to constant mass produces an anhydrous compound.
- The simplest ratio of the number of moles of the anhydrous compound to the number of moles of water determines the degree of hydration.

Summary

Atomic structure

Basics of atomic structure

Atoms are composed of three subatomic particles: protons, neutrons and electrons.

In all of the following sections the term 'relative' is used. It is used as a comparison between particles as the masses and charges of these particles are so small that it is easier to use standard measures and compare the rest to them (see Table 8).

Table 8

Subatomic particle	Relative mass	Relative charge	Location in atom
Proton	1	+1	Nucleus
Neutron	1	0	Nucleus
Electron	$\dfrac{1}{1840}$	−1	Shells (Energy levels)

Atoms with the same number of protons but a different number of neutrons are called **isotopes**. Isotopes have the same atomic number but a different mass number.

- The atomic number of an element is the same as the number of protons in the nucleus of the atom.
- The mass number of a particular atom is the total number of protons and neutrons in the nucleus of the atom.
- Relative atomic mass (RAM) is the average mass of the isotopes of an atom balanced in the proportions in which they occur relative to one-twelfth the mass of an atom of carbon-12.
- Relative isotopic mass (RIM) is the mass of an **isotope** of an element relative to one-twelfth the mass of an atom of carbon-12.
- Relative molecular mass is the mass of one molecule relative to one-twelfth the mass of an atom of carbon-12.

The atomic number is often called the proton number. The relative molecular mass is calculated from the total of all the relative atomic masses within a single molecule. The term relative formula mass (RFM) is used for all as it represents the mass of one formula unit relative to one-twelfth the mass of an atom of carbon-12.

The number of subatomic particles in an atom or ion can be determined from the atomic number, mass number and the charge on the particle. The atomic number is always the same as the number of protons in the nucleus.

The mass number is the total of the number of protons and the number of neutrons; so subtracting the atomic number from the mass number gives the number of neutrons in an atom or an ion.

Atoms are electrically neutral as they have equal numbers of protons and electrons. Simple ions are charged particles formed when atoms lose or gain electrons. The number of electrons subtracted from the number of protons gives the charge. Remember that an atom has no overall charge.

Number of protons = atomic number

Number of neutrons = mass number – atomic number

Charge = number of protons – number of electrons

Chlorine has two isotopes: chlorine-35 and chlorine-37. These are often written ^{35}Cl and ^{37}Cl. The relative atomic mass of chlorine is an average mass of the atoms, taking the proportions in which they occur into account. 75% of all chlorine atoms are ^{35}Cl and 25% are ^{37}Cl.

Examiner tip

It is the atomic number that defines the identity of the particle. A particle with 17 protons is always a chlorine particle — it may be a chlorine atom or a chloride ion depending on the number of electrons.

Examiner tip

The symbol for an element may be written with its atomic number and mass number, i.e. $^{A}_{Z}E$ where E is the symbol for the element, Z is the atomic number and A is the mass number, e.g. $^{35}_{17}$Cl, $^{37}_{17}$Cl, $^{12}_{6}$C. For isotopes, often the atomic number is left out, e.g. ^{35}Cl and ^{37}Cl.

The relative atomic mass of an element can be calculated from the relative isotopic masses of the isotopes (which are the same as the mass numbers) and the relative proportions in which they occur (relative abundance).

$$RAM = \frac{\sum(\text{mass of isotope} \times \text{relative abundance})}{\sum \text{relative abundance}}$$

where Σ represents the 'sum of' for all isotopes.

Worked example 1

Chlorine exists as two isotopes, ^{35}Cl and ^{37}Cl, which occur in the relative proportions 75% and 25% respectively. Calculate the relative atomic mass of chlorine.

$$RAM = \frac{(35 \times 75) + (37 \times 25)}{100} = \frac{3550}{100} = 35.5$$

Worked example 2

Determine the number of subatomic particles present in an aluminium ion, Al^{3+}.

From the Periodic Table, the atomic number of aluminium is 13 and the relative atomic mass is 27. Apart from chlorine (relative atomic mass 35.5), the relative atomic mass can be taken as the mass number of the most common isotope.

Number of protons = atomic number

Number of protons = 13

Number of neutrons = mass number – atomic number

Number of neutrons = 27 – 13 = 14

Charge = number of protons – number of electrons

+3 = 13 – number of electrons

Number of electrons = 13 – (+3) = 10

> **Knowledge check 5**
>
> State the relative charge and mass of an electron, a proton and a neutron.

Mass spectrometry

A mass spectrometer is an analytical instrument used to determine the mass of atoms and molecules. A mass spectrometer atomises and ionises a sample, producing ions with a single positive charge. It is assumed that all the ions in a mass spectrum have a single positive charge. The data obtained from a mass spectrometer can be for an element or a compound.

If the data are for an element, the spectrum will show the masses and relative abundances for all the isotopes of the element. These data can be supplied in the form of a table or a mass spectrum, which has peaks that show the relative abundance of each of the isotopes.

> **Examiner tip**
>
> Check the question for the number of decimal places and answer accordingly.

Worked example 1

An element was analysed using a mass spectrometer. The spectrum showed that there were four isotopes. The relative isotopic masses and relative abundances are given below.

Relative isotopic mass	Relative abundance
50	9
52	100
53	20
54	5

Calculate the relative atomic mass of the element to one decimal place.

This is carried out by thinking that in this sample 9 atoms have a mass of 50, 100 atoms have a mass of 52, 20 atoms have a mass of 53 and 5 atoms have a mass of 54. The relative atomic mass is simply the average mass of the atoms in the sample.

$$RAM = \frac{(9 \times 50) + (100 \times 52) + (20 \times 53) + (5 \times 54)}{9 + 100 + 20 + 5} = \frac{6980}{134} = 52.1 \text{ to } 1 \text{ d.p.}$$

These data could have been supplied in a spectrum such as the one shown in Figure 9, with peaks at 50, 52, 53 and 54 of the heights shown as the relative abundance. The calculation is the same.

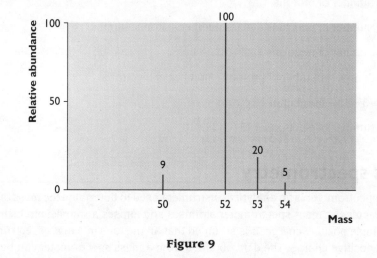

Figure 9

The horizontal axis of a mass spectrum can be labelled 'mass' or 'mass-to-charge ratio' or 'm/e' or 'm/z' but it is still mass. The vertical axis can be relative abundance or percentage abundance. If the relative abundance axis is not clear enough to read, the values will be supplied above the peaks.

You can be asked to identify the species that causes the peak at a particular mass value. For example, the peak at 54 in the mass spectrum is caused by $^{54}Cr^+$.

Remember to include the mass number; all species are assumed to have a single positive charge.

For a compound the mass spectrum is more complicated as the molecule breaks up during the process. The last major peak in the mass spectrum of a compound is called the **molecular ion** peak. The mass value for the molecular ion peak is the same as the RMM of the compound. The pattern seen below the molecular ion peak is called the fragmentation pattern and each peak is caused by a fragment of the molecule with a single positive charge.

The **molecular ion** is the ion formed by the removal of one electron from a molecule.

Figure 10 shows the spectrum for the compound ethanol, C_2H_5OH:

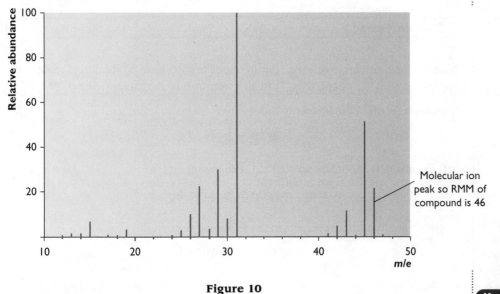

Figure 10

The species responsible for the peak at 46 is $C_2H_5OH^+$. The tallest peak in any mass spectrum is called the base peak.

Electronic configuration

Electrons are arranged in energy levels (the equivalent of shells) in which the energy of the electrons increases with increasing distance from the nucleus. The energy levels are labelled $n = 1$ (closest to the nucleus), $n = 2$, $n = 3$ etc. Energy levels are subdivided into subshells, which are made up of orbitals. Each orbital can be occupied by two electrons.

- An 's subshell' is made up of one s orbital.
- A 'p subshell' is made up of three p orbitals.
- A 'd subshell' is made up of five d orbitals.

At $n = 1$ there is only an s subshell, at $n = 2$ there is an s subshell and a p subshell and at $n = 3$ there is an s subshell, a p subshell and a d subshell. There is a fourth subshell called an f subshell, but this is not required at this level. (See Table 9.)

Table 9 The four types of orbital — s, p, d, f

Type	Shape	Start at which energy level	Number of this type of orbital in a subshell	Maximum number of electrons
s	Spherical	1	1	2
p	Dumbbell	2	3	6
d	Not required	3	5	10
f	Not required	4	7	14

Examiner tip
A common question is to be asked to sketch the shape of an s orbital or a p orbital — make sure you know these shapes, as this is an easy mark to obtain.

In each single orbital, electrons spin in opposite directions to minimise repulsions. Opposite spin is represented as: ↑↓ in 'electron-in-box' diagrams — see p. 29.

The subshells fill in the following order:

$$1s\ 2s\ 2p\ 3s\ 3p\ 4s\ 3d\ 4p$$

but the subshells should be written in the following order:

$$1s\ 2s\ 2p\ 3s\ 3p\ 3d\ 4s\ 4p$$

Electrons are lost from subshells in the following order:

$$4p\ 4s\ 3d\ 3p\ 3s\ 2p\ 2s\ 1s$$

Examiner tip
Remember that transition metal atoms lose their 4s electrons first. A common question is to ask for the electronic configuration of a transition metal ion.

The 2+ ion for transition metals is the most common and this is caused by loss of $4s^2$ electrons (not $3d$).

Determining electronic configuration of atoms and ions

An iron atom
- Atomic number of iron = 26, so an iron atom has 26 protons.
- Atoms are electrically neutral, so an atom of iron has 26 electrons.
- Using order of filling: $1s^2\ 2s^2\ 2p^6\ 3s^2\ 3p^6\ 4s^2\ 3d^6$
- Remember that when writing the order, the $4s$ has to come after the $3d$.
- So the electronic configuration of an iron atom is: $1s^2\ 2s^2\ 2p^6\ 3s^2\ 3p^6\ 3d^6\ 4s^2$.

An iron(II) ion
- The electronic configuration of an iron atom: $1s^2\ 2s^2\ 2p^6\ 3s^2\ 3p^6\ 3d^6\ 4s^2$
- Remember that transition metal atoms lose their $4s$ electrons first.
- An iron atom loses two electrons to form a 2+ ion.
- So the electronic configuration of an iron(II) ion is: $1s^2\ 2s^2\ 2p^6\ 3s^2\ 3p^6\ 3d^6$

A bromide ion, Br^-
- The electronic configuration of a bromine atom is determined first.
- The atomic number of bromine = 35 so a Br atom has 35 protons and 35 electrons.

- The electronic configuration of a Br atom: $1s^2\ 2s^2\ 2p^6\ 3s^2\ 3p^6\ 3d^{10}\ 4s^2\ 4p^5$
- A bromine atom gains one electron to form a bromide ion.
- The electronic configuration of a bromide ion is: $1s^2\ 2s^2\ 2p^6\ 3s^2\ 3p^6\ 3d^{10}\ 4s^2\ 4p^6$

The electronic configurations of chromium and copper atoms are unusual:

Cr: $1s^2\ 2s^2\ 2p^6\ 3s^2\ 3p^6\ 3d^5\ 4s^1$ (NOT $3d^4\ 4s^2$)

Cu: $1s^2\ 2s^2\ 2p^6\ 3s^2\ 3p^6\ 3d^{10},\ 4s^1$ (NOT $3d^9\ 4s^2$)

Note: Cr and Cu have unusual electronic configurations due to the stability of the half-filled and filled d^5 and d^{10} configurations. However, the formation of ions of copper and chromium works in the normal way with the loss of the $4s$ electrons first.

There are three main blocks in the Periodic Table. The blocks are based on the subshell in which the outer electrons are located (Figure 11).

Examiner tip

As soon as you start any AS or A2 exam, put a star (*) at Cr and Cu on your Periodic Table to remind you that their electronic configurations are different from what you would expect. This can be asked in any AS or A2 unit.

s block
(as outer electrons are in the s subshell)

d block
(as outer electrons are in the d subshell)

p block
(as outer electrons are in the p subshell)

Figure 11 Blocks of the Periodic Table

'Electron-in-box' diagrams

The electronic configuration can be asked for in written format or in an 'electron-in-box' form. Electrons only pair when no other space is available in the subshell. Electrons in a subshell that are not paired spin in the same direction and are represented by arrows pointing in the same direction.

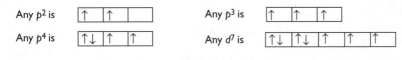

Figure 12

Often something like Figure 12 is used. Sometimes you have to label the subshells so you will have to be able to identify and label $1s$, $2s$, $2p$ etc. It is relatively easy as the s subshell has only one orbital, the p subshell has three orbitals and the d subshell has five orbitals. Also, there is an s subshell at each energy level; there is a p subshell at each energy level except $n = 1$; there is a d subshell at each energy level except $n = 1$ and $n = 2$. Remember that the $4s$ is at a slightly lower energy level than the $3d$.

When filling the subshells remember to start at the lowest and work up. Also remember that for p and d subshells there should only be 1 electron in each orbital until each is half-filled and then start pairing electrons in orbitals.

Finally, remember that electrons are shown as arrows pointing up ($\uparrow$) and arrows pointing down ($\downarrow$). The opposite directions represent the different directions of spin of the electrons in one orbital. All the first set of electrons in one subshell should be in the same direction.

Worked examples

A nitrogen atom (atomic number 7)

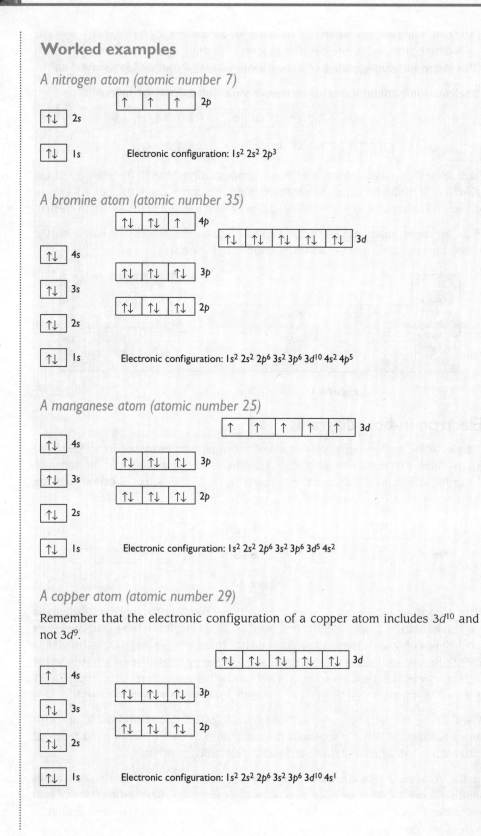

Electronic configuration: $1s^2\ 2s^2\ 2p^3$

A bromine atom (atomic number 35)

Electronic configuration: $1s^2\ 2s^2\ 2p^6\ 3s^2\ 3p^6\ 3d^{10}\ 4s^2\ 4p^5$

A manganese atom (atomic number 25)

Electronic configuration: $1s^2\ 2s^2\ 2p^6\ 3s^2\ 3p^6\ 3d^5\ 4s^2$

A copper atom (atomic number 29)

Remember that the electronic configuration of a copper atom includes $3d^{10}$ and not $3d^9$.

Electronic configuration: $1s^2\ 2s^2\ 2p^6\ 3s^2\ 3p^6\ 3d^{10}\ 4s^1$

An iron(III) ion

The electronic configuration of an iron atom is: $1s^2\ 2s^2\ 2p^6\ 3s^2\ 3p^6\ 3d^6\ 4s^2$

The electronic configuration of an iron(III) ion is: $1s^2\ 2s^2\ 2p^6\ 3s^2\ 3p^6\ 3d^5$

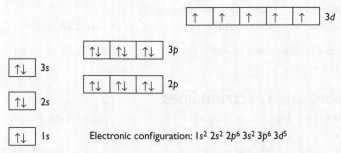

Electronic configuration: $1s^2\ 2s^2\ 2p^6\ 3s^2\ 3p^6\ 3d^5$

You may be given all subshells in an 'electron-in-box' style question up to and including $4p$, but you may only need to use some of them.

Atomic emission and absorption spectroscopy

Atomic spectroscopy examines gaseous atoms. It shows evidence for the existence of discrete energy levels and also that the energy levels get closer together moving out from the nucleus.

Figure 13 is a representation of the emission spectrum for atomic hydrogen.

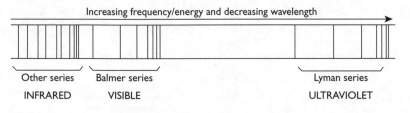

Figure 13 Emission spectrum for hydrogen

In the infrared region, three series are found and they overlap. They are called the Pfund, Brackett and Paschen series. Brackett overlaps with both the Pfund and the Paschen series.

Key points to note on the spectrum:
- The spectrum is made up of discrete lines — it is not continuous.
- As energy/frequency increases within a series, the spectral lines get closer together.

Emission spectroscopy examines the energy released when electrons fall back to lower energy levels.

Absorption spectroscopy examines the energy taken in when electrons are excited to higher energy levels. '**Ground state**' is used to describe an atom or ion where all the electrons are in the lowest possible energy levels.

Excitation of electrons occurs when electrons are given energy and move to higher energy levels further from the nucleus.

Examiner tip

Remember that transition metal atoms lose their 4s electrons first.

Knowledge check 7

Explain why magnesium is described as being an s block element.

Transition is the general term used for the movement of electrons between energy levels.

The presence of discrete lines in an emission spectrum is explained by:
(1) electrons excited to higher discrete energy levels
(2) electrons falling back down to lower discrete energy levels
(3) energy emitted as ultraviolet, visible and infrared electromagnetic radiation

The convergence of the discrete lines is due to the energy levels becoming closer together further from the nucleus.

Electron transitions and spectrum lines

- Emission lines in the infrared region are caused by electron transitions from higher levels to $n = 3, 4, 5, 6$
- Emission lines in the visible region are caused by electron transitions from higher levels to $n = 2$.
- Emission lines in the ultraviolet region are caused by electron transition from higher levels to $n = 1$.

The size of electron transition is proportional to the frequency of emitted/absorbed radiation and is also proportional to the energy of emitted/absorbed radiation.

Specific spectral lines

For a specific line in a spectrum you will have to identify the electronic transition responsible. Working out the two levels involved in the transition is the same for both emission spectroscopy and absorption spectroscopy; you simply make the arrow go down for emission spectroscopy and up for absorption spectroscopy (Figure 14).

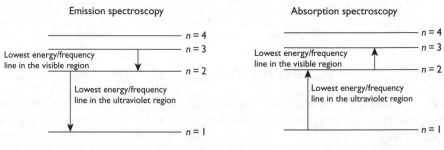

Figure 14

Calculating energy changes from frequency and wavelength

Frequency can be converted to energy using the expression: $E = h \times f$
- E = energy (measured in joules, J)
- h = Planck's constant (6.63×10^{-34} Js)
- f = frequency (measured in Hertz, Hz — sometimes written s^{-1})

Frequency and wavelength are linked by the expression: $c = f \times \lambda$
- where c is the speed of light (3×10^8 m s^{-1})
- f is frequency measured in Hz
- λ is wavelength measured in m

Examiner tip
Often wavelength is given in nanometres (nm), which is $\times 10^{-9}$ m.

Worked example 1

Determine the energy in joules for red light that has a wavelength of 675 nm.

Convert nm to m: $675 \text{ nm} = 675 \times 10^{-9} \text{ m}$

Calculate frequency from wavelength: $c = f \times \lambda$, where $c = 3 \times 10^8 \text{ ms}^{-1}$:

$$3 \times 10^8 = f \times 675 \times 10^{-9}$$

$$f = \frac{3 \times 10^8}{675 \times 10^{-9}} = 4.44 \times 10^{14} \text{ Hz}$$

Calculating energy from frequency:

$$E = h \times f$$

$$E = 6.63 \times 10^{-34} \times 4.44 \times 10^{14} = 2.944 \times 10^{-19} \text{ J}$$

Converting convergence limit to ionisation energy

The convergence limit is an imaginary line in an emission spectrum beyond the last line in the ultraviolet region, where the lines would appear to converge. The frequency of the convergence limit corresponds to the ionisation of an atom and can be used to calculate the ionisation energy of the atom in kJ mol^{-1} using the following steps:

(1) Use $E = h \times f$, so multiply frequency of the convergence limit by Planck's constant to give energy in J (essentially this is J/atom).
(2) Multiply the answer to step 1 by Avogadro's constant (N_A) to give energy in J/mol.
(3) Divide the answer to step 2 by 1000 to give energy in kJ mol^{-1}

Worked example 2

The frequency of the convergence limit for atomic hydrogen is found at a frequency of $3.287 \times 10^{15} \text{ Hz}$. Calculate the first ionisation energy of hydrogen.

Step 1   Convert frequency to energy using $E = h \times f$.
$$E = 6.63 \times 10^{-34} \times 3.287 \times 10^{15}$$
$$E = 2.179 \times 10^{-18} \text{ J}$$

Step 2   Convert to J/mol by multiplying by Avogadro's number (N_A).
$$E = 2.179 \times 10^{-18} \times 6.02 \times 10^{23}$$
$$E = 1.312 \times 10^6 \text{ J/mol}$$

Step 3   Convert to kJ/mol by dividing by 1000.
$$E = 1.312 \times 10^6 / 1000$$
$$E = 1312 \text{ kJ mol}^{-1}$$

Examiner tip
This type of calculation can be from the frequency of any spectral line, and you may be asked to calculate the energy associated with this line in kJ mol^{-1}. The calculation is the same. A question may only require the calculation of energy in J, in which case only carry out step 1.

The flame test

A flame test can identify metal ions present in an ionic compound. It is carried out using a piece of nichrome wire. Concentrated hydrochloric acid must be used with nichrome wire.

- Dip the end of a piece of nichrome wire in concentrated hydrochloric acid.
- Dip the end of the wire in the sample.
- Place the sample in a blue Bunsen flame.
- Observe the flame colour.

The concentrated hydrochloric acid cleans the nichrome wire and also makes it wet so the sample will stick to the wire. If the ionic compound is not a chloride, the concentrated hydrochloric acid forms the chloride. Chlorides are more volatile in a Bunsen flame.

Flame test results

- Lilac flame = K^+ present (pink when viewed through cobalt blue glass)
- Yellow/orange flame = Na^+ present
- Crimson flame = Li^+ present
- Green flame = Ba^{2+} present
- Brick red flame = Ca^{2+} present
- Blue-green flame = Cu^{2+} present

The ions present cause characteristic flame colours because electrons are excited to higher energy levels and as they fall back to lower energy levels, energy is emitted as visible light.

Ionisation energy

Values of ionisation energies are always endothermic and always measured in $kJ\,mol^{-1}$.

- **First ionisation energy** is the energy required to remove 1 mol of electrons from 1 mol of gaseous atoms to form 1 mol of gaseous monopositive ions.
- **Second ionisation energy** is the energy required to remove 1 mol of electrons from 1 mol of gaseous monopositive ions to form 1 mol of gaseous dipositive ions.
- **Third ionisation energy** is the energy required to remove 1 mol of electrons from 1 mol of gaseous dipositive ions to form 1 mol of gaseous tripositive ions.

In the following example, X represents any element.

Equation for first ionisation energy:

$$X(g) \rightarrow X^+(g) + e^-$$

Equation for second ionisation energy:

$$X^+(g) \rightarrow X^{2+}(g) + e^-$$

Equation for third ionisation energy:

$$X^{2+}(g) \rightarrow X^{3+}(g) + e^-$$

$X(g) \rightarrow X^{2+}(g) + 2e^-$ would be a combination of the first and second ionisation energies. The value for this would be the first and second ionisation energies added together, for example:

Examiner tip

The origin of flame colours is a common question. Learn the flame test colours carefully as no other colours are accepted.

Examiner tip

Remember that only one colour from a list separated by a slash (/) will be accepted. A hyphen (-) means both colours are required separated by a hyphen. Never use a slash (/) when answering colours of chemicals.

Knowledge check 8

Explain how a flame test colour arises.

Examiner tip

Equations for ionisation energy must have *gaseous* species (atoms or ions) and only 1 mole of electrons removed each time. The electrons do not require a state symbol.

First ionisation energy of magnesium = +740 kJ mol^{-1}

This is for the change $Mg(g) \rightarrow Mg^+(g) + e^-$

Second ionisation energy of magnesium = +1500 kJ mol^{-1}

This is for the change $Mg^+(g) \rightarrow Mg^{2+}(g) + e^-$

The energy for the change $Mg(g) \rightarrow Mg^{2+}(g) + 2e^-$ = +740 + 1500 = +2240 kJ

Patterns in first ionisation energy

Figure 15 shows the change in first ionisation energies from hydrogen (atomic number 1) to krypton (atomic number 36).

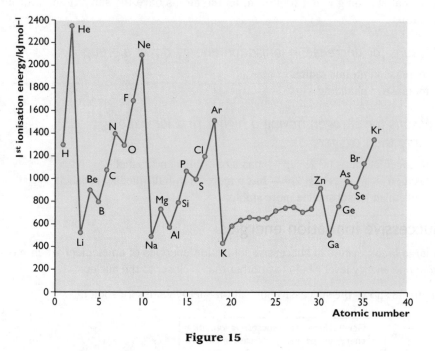

Figure 15

Identifying elements

The elements that have the lowest first ionisation energy in each period are the alkali metals (Group I).

The elements that have the highest first ionisation energy in each period are the noble gases (Group VIII or 0).

Factors used to explain changes in ionisation energy

The following four factors are used to explain trends in ionisation energies:
(1) nuclear charge
(2) atomic radius
(3) shielding (by inner electrons)
(4) stability of filled and half-filled subshells

Trends seen in the graph of first ionisation energies

- Across a period — first ionisation energy generally increases.
- Down a group — first ionisation energy decreases.

Note that elements in Groups II, V and 0 exhibit higher than expected first ionisation energy values, due to the stability of half-filled and filled subshells.

Reasons for increase in ionisation energy across a period

- Increase in nuclear charge
- Decrease in atomic radius

Note that shielding is not important as the atoms have the same number of inner electrons.

Reasons for decrease in ionisation energy down a group

- Increase in atomic radius
- Increase in shielding

Reasons for nitrogen having a higher first ionisation energy than oxygen

- Nitrogen atom — $1s^2 2s^2 2p^3$ — has a half-filled $2p$ subshell.
- Oxygen atom — $1s^2 2s^2 2p^4$ — has a more-than-half-filled $2p$ subshell.
- Half-filled $2p$ subshell is more stable.

Successive ionisation energies

A large break occurs in successive ionisation energies of an element when moving from one energy level (shell) to another that is closer to the nucleus.

Figure 16 shows the successive ionisation energy values for sodium.

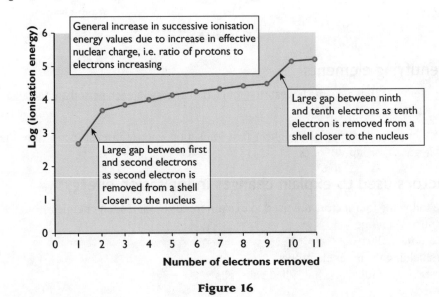

Figure 16

Examiner tip

With the half-filled (Group V) and filled (Groups II and 0) subshells, always state the electronic configuration of the atoms involved and then explain about the stability. For example: a phosphorus atom is $1s^2 2s^2 2p^6 3s^2 3p^3$; the half-filled $3p$ subshell is more stable.

Examiner tip

If you are asked to sketch a graph of successive ionisation energy values for a particular element, remember to do it from the outer electrons to the inner. For example at GCSE sodium is 2,8,1, but the successive graph should show 1 electron (large gap) then 8 electrons (large gap) and finally 2 electrons. The graph should be constantly increasing.

The log scale is used as there is such a large difference in ionisation values that it would be impossible to plot on a conventional scale. For example, the first ionisation energy of sodium is $+500\,kJ\,mol^{-1}$ but the eleventh ionisation energy is $+158\,700\,kJ\,mol^{-1}$.

Often a question may give successive ionisation energies for some elements and ask you to determine the element in a particular group of the Periodic Table. Look for the large jump in successive ionisation energies. This jump occurs after all the outer shell electrons have been removed and will indicate the number of electrons in the outer shell.

Worked example

An element has the following successive ionisation energies:

Ionisation energy	First	Second	Third	Fourth	Fifth	Sixth
kJ mol^{-1}	580	1800	2700	11 600	14 800	18 400

The large jump in successive ionisation energy values occurs after three electrons are removed so there must be three electrons in the outer shell, which would indicate a Group III element.

You may be asked to work out the formula of a compound of this element, for example write the formula of the oxide of the element using M to represent the element; use simple valency rules to determine the oxide to be M_2O_3, as M is in Group III.

Knowledge check 9

State the four factors that affect ionisation energies.

- Atoms are composed of protons, neutrons and electrons. Electrons have a much smaller mass than protons and neutrons. Protons have a relative charge of +1 and electrons −1; neutrons have no charge.
- Mass spectrometry measures the masses of particles in a sample, based on each having a single positive charge.
- For an element, mass spectrometry measures the mass and relative abundance of each isotope of the element.
- Elements can be classified as s block, p block or d block, depending on which subshell their outer shell electrons are found in.

- The first series of transition metal atoms lose their 4s electrons first.
- The first ionisation energy is the energy required to remove one mole of electrons from one mole of gaseous atoms to form one mole of gaseous monopositive ions.
- First ionisation energies increase across a period but decrease down a group.
- The four factors that are used to explain patterns in ionisation energies are: atomic radius, nuclear charge, shielding by inner electrons and stability of filled and half-filled subshells.

Summary

Bonding and structure

All pure substances may be classified as elements or compounds. Figure 17 shows the main subdivisions of all pure substances. The type of bonding and structure shown by each type of substance with some common examples are also given.

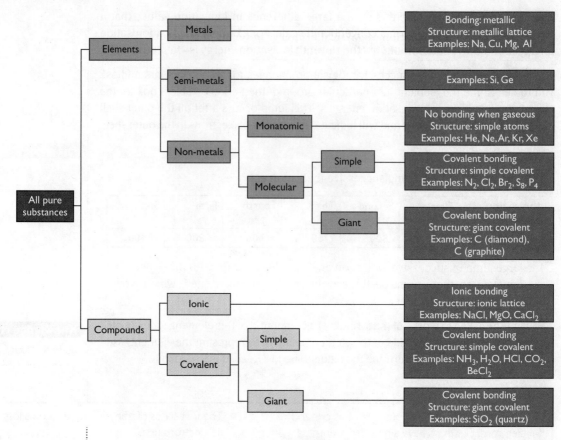

Figure 17

State the type of bonding found in calcium chloride.

Each type of structure (metals, ionic compounds, giant covalent structures and simple covalent structures) will be examined. Semi-metals can also be called metalloids and they have properties of both metals and non-metals. Silicon has a giant covalent structure.

Metals

Metal bonding (Figure 18) involves layers of positive ions held together by a sea of delocalised electrons (outer shell electrons, which do not occupy fixed positions but move freely in the structure). The structure is a metallic lattice. Physical properties of metals are listed in Table 10.

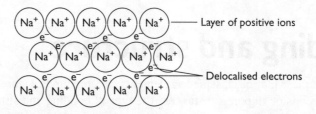

Figure 18 Typical diagram showing metallic bonding

CCEA AS Chemistry

Table 10 Physical properties of metals related to bonding and structure

Physical property	Explanation of physical property in terms of structure and bonding
Hardness	Strong attraction between positive ions and negative electrons, and a regular structure
High melting point	Large amount of energy is required to break the bonds, which are strong attractions between positive ions and negative electrons
Good electrical conductivity	Delocalised electrons can move and carry charge through the metal
Malleability and ductility	Layers of positive ions can slide over each other without disrupting the bonding

Knowledge check 11
What is meant by metallic bonding?

Ionic compounds

Ionic bonding is the electrostatic attraction of oppositely charged ions in a regular, ionic lattice. The structure of an ionic compound is described as an ionic lattice. A lattice is a regular arrangement of particles, in this case positive and negative ions.

Ionic compounds are generally compounds containing a metal, particularly a Group I or II metal, and a non-metal, particularly a Group VI or VII non-metal.

Positive ions are called cations and negative ions are called anions. Simple cations have the same name as the parent atom, e.g. sodium ion, Na^+; hydrogen ion, H^+; aluminium ion, Al^{3+}. Simple anions have an -ide ending, e.g. oxide, O^{2-}; chloride, Cl^-; hydride, H^-; nitride, N^{3-}. All simple ions have a noble gas electronic configuration.

Other common simple cations found in ionic compounds include: silver(I), Ag^+; copper(II), Cu^{2+}; iron(II), Fe^{2+}; iron(III), Fe^{3+}; nickel(II), Ni^{2+}; cobalt(II), Co^{2+}; zinc, Zn^{2+}; manganese(II), Mn^{2+}.

Positive molecular ions end in -onium. The most common molecular ion is the ammonium ion, NH_4^+, but you will also come across the hydroxonium ion, H_3O^+.

Negative molecular ions usually end in -ate. However, some common names end in -ite.

Other common molecular anions found in ionic compounds include: sulfate ion, SO_4^{2-}; carbonate ion, CO_3^{2-}; nitrate ion, NO_3^-; hydroxide, OH^-; hypochlorite, OCl^-; hydrogencarbonate, HCO_3^-; dichromate or dichromate(VI), $Cr_2O_7^{2-}$; permanganate or manganate(VII), MnO_4^-.

Examiner tip
There are a few negative molecular ions that end in -ide. Examples are hydroxide, OH^- and cyanide, CN^-. Remember these, as they are unusual.

Dot-and-cross diagrams

Ionic compounds are formed when metal atoms transfer electrons to non-metal atoms. A dot-and-cross diagram can be used to show how the electrons are transferred:

- Only outer shell electrons are shown on all atoms and ions.
- The correct number of each atom required must be shown, together with the correct number of each ion in the compound.
- Ions should be placed in square brackets with the transferred electrons shown in the ions (using × or •) and the charge on all the ions should be shown outside the brackets. Figure 19 shows an example.

Examiner tip
Remember that the formula of an ionic compound can be worked out using the charges on the ions: e.g. ammonium carbonate contains NH_4^+ and CO_3^{2-} ions. Two ammonium ions are required to cancel out the charge on the carbonate ion, so the formula of ammonium carbonate is $(NH_4)_2CO_3$.

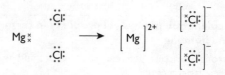

Figure 19 Magnesium chloride

- For the formation of any ionic compound, always show the outer shell electrons in the atoms using a cross (×) for the electrons in one type of atom and a dot (•) for the electrons in the other type of atom. Then show the outer shell electrons in the ions. Make sure that any transferred electrons remain as × or •. This allows the source of the electrons to be seen clearly (Figure 20).

$$Ca_{\times}^{\times} \quad \cdot\ddot{O}: \quad \longrightarrow \quad \left[Ca\right]^{2+} \quad \left[{}_{\times}^{\times}\ddot{O}:\right]^{2-}$$

Figure 20 Calcium oxide

Properties of ionic compounds are given in Table 11.

Table 11 Properties of ionic compounds related to bonding and structure

Physical property	Explanation of physical property in terms of structure and bonding
Crystalline	Regular lattice of positive and negative ions. Regular arrangement creates crystal structure
High melting point and boiling point	Large amount of energy is required to break the bonds which are strong electrostatic attractions between ions of opposite charge
Non-conductor of electricity when solid	Ions are not free to move and cannot carry charge
Good conductor of electricity when molten or when aqueous (dissolved in water)	Ions are free to move and can carry charge

Covalent bonding

- A single covalent bond is a shared pair of electrons. Normally each atom provides one electron. A single covalent bond is represented as a line between two atoms, e.g. H–Cl.
- A double covalent bond is two shared pairs of electrons. A double covalent bond is represented as a double line between two atoms, e.g. O=C=O.
- A triple covalent bond is three shared pairs of electrons. A triple covalent bond is represented as a triple line between two atoms, e.g. N≡N.

Covalent bonds exist between non-metal atoms (some exceptions occur where metal atoms can form covalent bonds, e.g. Be in $BeCl_2$ and Al in $AlCl_3$). Dot-and-cross diagrams are again used to show the arrangement of electrons in covalently bonded molecules. A shared pair of electrons can be represented as ×• to show that the two electrons in the bond are from different atoms (Figure 21).

Knowledge check 12

What is meant by a single covalent bond?

Dot-and-cross diagrams for common molecules with single covalent bonds

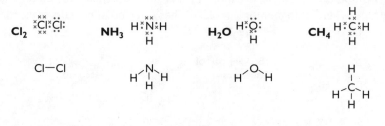

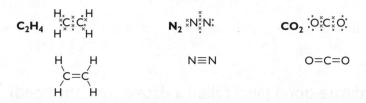

Dot-and-cross diagrams for common molecules with multiple covalent bonds

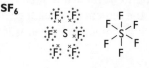

Figure 21

The 'octet rule' states that when forming a compound, an atom tends to gain, lose or share electrons to achieve eight electrons in its outer shell. Some molecules have atoms that deviate from the octet rule. They are said to have contracted their octet (i.e. have fewer than eight electrons in their outer shell) or expanded their octet (i.e. have more than eight electrons in their outer shell) — see Figure 22.

Common examples of contraction of octet

BeCl$_2$:Cl×Be×Cl:

Cl—Be—Cl

BF$_3$:F:
          :F× B
             :F:

F   F
 \   /
  B
  |
  F

Common example of expansion of octet

SF$_6$:F: :F:
          :F× S ×F:
          :F: :F:

   F
F \ | / F
   S
F / | \ F
   F

Figure 22

Often questions ask you to explain how certain atoms obey or do not obey the octet rule. State the octet rule and then which atoms obey it (or not) and explain how by stating the number of electrons in their outer shell. For example, in beryllium chloride, BeCl$_2$, the Be atom does not obey the octet rule as it has only four electrons in its outer shell whereas the octet rule states there should be eight electrons in the outer shell.

Knowledge check 13

Does carbon in methane obey the octet rule? Explain your answer.

Bonding pairs of electrons and lone pairs of electrons

A **bonding pair of electrons** is a pair of electrons shared between two atoms. A **lone pair of electrons** is an unshared (unbonded) pair of electrons in the outer shell of an atom. For example, in a molecule like methane there are four bonding pairs of electrons, whereas an ammonia molecule has three bonding pairs of electrons and one lone pair of electrons (Figure 23).

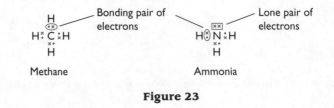

Figure 23

The number of bonding pairs of electrons and lone pairs of electrons helps determine the shape of a molecule but is also important for the formation of a coordinate bond.

Coordinate bond (also called a dative covalent bond)

A coordinate bond is a covalent bond where the shared pair of electrons are both donated from one atom. Note that when a coordinate bond forms, a lone pair of electrons becomes a bonding pair of electrons. There are many examples of coordinate bonded ions.

Note that in a coordinate bonded ion the charge must be shown, for example the ammonium ion, NH_4^+ (Figure 24).

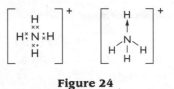

Figure 24

In the dot-and-cross diagram, the coordinate bond is shown with two crosses to show that the two electrons come from the same atom. It is also shown as an arrow in the bonding diagram, with the direction indicating where the two electrons come from. Note that once a coordinate bond is formed it is exactly the same as a covalent bond.

Molecular covalent crystals

There are two main examples of molecular covalent crystals: sulfur and iodine. The forces of attraction between simple covalent molecules are usually so weak that they are gases, liquids or, at best, low-melting-point solids. When they are solid, many form molecular covalent crystals.

Sulfur exists as S_8 molecules, which consist of eight sulfur atoms covalently bonded together in a puckered ring. Iodine exists as a simple diatomic molecule, I_2 (Figure 25).

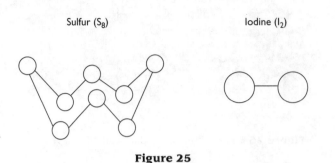

Sulfur (S_8) Iodine (I_2)

Figure 25

Properties of molecular covalent crystals linked to bonding and structure

Molecular covalent crystals usually have low melting/boiling points due to weak intermolecular forces. They do not conduct electricity in any state as they have no free electrons/ions to carry charge.

Giant covalent crystals

The two main examples of giant covalent (or macromolecular) crystals are carbon (graphite) and carbon (diamond). The strong covalent bonds between the atoms in these crystals mean that they are high-melting-point solids (a lot of energy is needed to break the strong covalent bonds). The regular structure means that they are crystalline.

In diamond each carbon atom is covalently bonded to four others in a tetrahedral arrangement (Figure 26a). The rigid three-dimensional structure of diamond combined with the strong covalent bonds means that it is hard.

In graphite each carbon is covalently bonded to three others in a layered hexagonal structure (Figure 26b). Between the layers there are delocalised electrons that can move and carry charge. Therefore, in the solid state graphite can conduct electricity. However, whereas molten metals continue to conduct electricity, molten graphite does not conduct electricity as the structure is disrupted. Diamond does not conduct electricity as there are no delocalised electrons to move and carry the charge.

Graphite can also act as a lubricant, as the layers can slide over each other due to the weak bonds between them (Figure 26b).

(a)   (b)

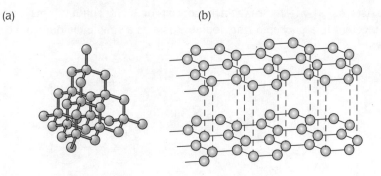

Figure 26 The structure of (a) diamond and (b) graphite

Electronegativity and polarity

Electronegativity is the numerical value of the ability of an atom to attract the bonding electrons in a covalent bond. In a covalent bond the two atoms at either end of the bond have an electronegativity value. For example in H–Cl the electronegativity values are: H = 2.1; Cl = 3.0.

This means that the electrons in this bond are drawn closer to Cl than to H as Cl has a higher electronegativity value. This is represented by the use of δ+ (delta plus) and δ– (delta minus) above the atoms in the bond. The δ– is placed above the atom that has the higher electronegativity value and the δ+ is placed above the atom with the lower electronegativity value (Figure 27). This covalent bond is now described as being polar.

$$\overset{\delta+ \quad \delta-}{H-Cl}$$

Figure 27

A polar bond is one where the atoms at either end of the bond have different electronegativity values resulting in an unequal sharing of the bonding electrons (Figure 28).

Examples of polar bonds: $\overset{\delta-}{O}-\overset{\delta+}{H}$ $\overset{\delta-}{N}-\overset{\delta+}{H}$ $\overset{\delta+}{H}-\overset{\delta-}{F}$ $\overset{\delta+}{C}=\overset{\delta-}{O}$

Examples of non-polar bonds: I–I   C–H   C=C   Cl–Cl

Figure 28

Trends in electronegativity

As a group is descended, electronegativity decreases (bonded electrons are further from the attractive power of the nucleus). As a period is crossed from left to right, electronegativity increases (as bonded electrons are closer to the attractive power of the nucleus).

The most electronegative element is fluorine. The least electronegative element that forms stable compounds is caesium.

Ionic and covalent character

For compounds composed of two different elements, the difference in electronegativity between the atoms of the elements dictates the type of compound formed (i.e. ionic or covalent) and, if the compound is covalent, also the polarity of the molecule.

- No/very small difference in electronegativity gives a non-polar molecule, for example: Br_2; I_2; Cl_2; O_2; CH_4.
- Small difference in electronegativity gives a polar molecule, for example: HF; HCl; H_2O; NH_3.
- Large difference in electronegativity = ionic compound, for example: NaCl; MgO; $CaBr_2$.

Simple covalent molecules can be polar or non-polar depending on whether or not they contain polar bonds, but also based on their shape.

If a molecule contains equally polar bonds arranged symmetrically then the polarity of the bonds cancel each other out and the molecule is non-polar, for example carbon dioxide, CO_2 is a linear molecule (Figure 29).

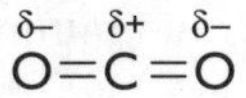

$$\overset{\delta-}{O}=\overset{\delta+}{C}=\overset{\delta-}{O}$$

Figure 29 Equal polar bonds are arranged symmetrically, so the bond polarities cancel each other out

Knowledge check 14

Explain which is more electronegative, chlorine or iodine.

- Substances are either pure or mixtures.
- Pure substances are either elements or compounds; elements are either metals or non-metals (or semi-metals).
- Metals exhibit metallic bonding (positive ions held together by a field of delocalised electrons).
- Most compounds containing a metal exhibit ionic bonding (attractions between oppositely charged ions); exceptions are $BeCl_2$ and $AlCl_3$.
- Compounds containing only non-metals exhibit covalent bonding (sharing of electrons).
- Some non-metallic elements and compounds form simple molecules that exhibit covalent bonding.
- Some non-metallic elements and compounds exhibit covalent bonding, forming a giant lattice covalent bonding.
- Bonding and structure are different. Ionic, metallic and giant covalent substances have different bonding but have a lattice structure.
- The physical properties of substances can be explained in terms of their structure and bonding.
- Electronegativity is the ability of an atom in a covalent bond to attract the bonding electrons.
- Simple covalent molecules can be described as polar or non-polar based on the difference in electronegativity of the atoms involved and also the symmetry of the molecule.

Summary

Shapes of molecules

Valence shell electron pair repulsion theory

The shape of a covalent molecule depends on the repulsion of the electrons around an atom. The electron pairs around an atom repel each other. There are two types of electron pair, a bonding pair of electrons and a lone pair of electrons.

You must be able to identify the lone pairs and bonding pairs of electrons in any molecule. Lone pairs are closer to the central atom so they have a greater repulsive effect on the other pairs of electrons.

The order of strength of the repulsions experienced by the electron pairs is shown in Figure 30.

Lone pair ↔ Lone pair **LP↔LP**	is greater than	Lone pair ↔ Bonding pair **LP↔BP**	is greater than	Bonding pair ↔ Bonding pair **BP↔BP**

Figure 30

This means that lone pairs of electrons repel lone pairs of electrons more than they repel bonding pairs of electrons. The lowest level of repulsion is between bonding pairs of electrons.

Determining the shape of a molecule

(1) Draw a dot-and-cross diagram, showing how the electron pairs in the valence shell of the central atom are arranged.

(2) Draw the molecular shape that would minimise repulsions, bearing in mind the order of strength of repulsions.

(3) Describe the molecular shape in relation to how the atoms (not electron pairs) are arranged.

Stating and explaining the shape of a molecule

(1) State the number of lone pairs of electrons and bonding pairs of electrons.

(2) State that the 'electron pairs repel each other'.

(3) (a) If only bonding pairs of electrons are present, state that bonding pairs of electrons repel each other equally, *or*

(b) If both bonding pairs of electrons and lone pairs of electrons are present, state that lone pairs of electrons repel more than bonding pairs of electrons.

(4) State that the molecule takes up the shape to minimise repulsions.

(5) State the shape and the bond angle.

Examples with only bonding pairs of electrons

Beryllium chloride ($BeCl_2$ — Figure 31)

Be   Electronic configuration $1s^2\,2s^2$ [2, 2]

Cl   Electronic configuration $1s^2\,2s^2\,2p^6\,3s^2\,3p^5$ [2, 8, 7]

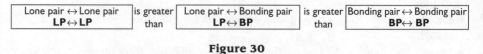

Figure 31 Beryllium chloride: bond angle is 180°; shape is linear

Explanation of shape:

- Electron pairs repel each other.
- Two bonding pairs of electrons repel each other equally.
- Molecule takes up shape to minimise repulsions.

Boron trifluoride (BF$_3$ — Figure 32)

B   Electronic configuration $1s^2\,2s^2\,2p^1$ [2, 3]

F   Electronic configuration $1s^2\,2s^2\,2p^5$ [2, 7]

Figure 32 Boron trifluoride: bond angle is 120°; shape is trigonal planar

Explanation of shape:
- Electron pairs repel each other.
- Three bonding pairs of electrons repel each other equally.
- Molecule takes up shape to minimise repulsions.

Methane (CH$_4$ — Figure 33)

C   Electronic configuration $1s^2\,2s^2\,2p^2$ [2, 4]

H   Electronic configuration $1s^1$ [1]

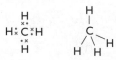

Figure 33 Methane: bond angle is 109.5°; shape is tetrahedral

Explanation of shape:
- Electron pairs repel each other.
- Four bonding pairs of electrons repel each other equally.
- Molecule takes up shape to minimise repulsions.

Carbon dioxide (CO$_2$ — Figure 34)

C   Electronic configuration $1s^2\,2s^2\,2p^2$ [2, 4]

O   Electronic configuration $1s^2\,2s^2\,2p^4$ [2, 6]

$$\ddot{\mathrm{O}} \overset{\times}{\underset{\times}{\mathrm{C}}} \ddot{\mathrm{O}} \qquad \mathrm{O=C=O}$$

Figure 34 Carbon dioxide: bond angle is 180°; shape is linear

Explanation of shape:
- Electron pairs repel each other.
- Two sets of bonding pairs of electrons repel each other equally.
- Molecule takes up shape to minimise repulsions.

Sulfur hexafluoride (SF$_6$ — Figure 35)

S   Electronic configuration $1s^2\,2s^2\,2p^6\,3s^2\,3p^4$ [2, 8, 6]

F   Electronic configuration $1s^2\,2s^2\,2p^5$ [2, 7]

Examiner tip

A double or a triple bond counts as one bonding pair of electrons when determining shape. Remember that the identical and symmetrical polar bonds explain the lack of polarity in the carbon dioxide molecule even though it contains polar bonds.

Knowledge check 15

State and explain the shape of methane, CH$_4$.

Figure 35 Sulfur hexafluoride: bond angle is 90°; shape is octahedral

Explanation of shape:
- Electron pairs repel each other.
- Six bonding pairs of electrons repel each other equally.
- Molecule takes up shape to minimise repulsions.

Examples with bonding pairs of electrons and lone pairs of electrons

The following examples all have *four* pairs of electrons around the central atom. These pairs of electrons take up a basic tetrahedral shape like methane (CH_4). However, out of the four pairs of electrons, some are bonding pairs and some are lone pairs, but remember that a lone pair of electrons has a greater repulsion than a bonding pair of electrons.

Ammonia (NH_3 — Figure 36)

N   Electronic configuration $1s^2\, 2s^2\, 2p^3$ [2, 5]

H   Electronic configuration $1s^1$ [1]

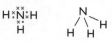

Figure 36 Ammonia: bond angle is 107°; shape is pyramidal

Explanation of shape:
- Electron pairs repel each other.
- Three bonding pairs of electrons and one lone pair of electrons.
- Lone pair of electrons has a greater repulsion.
- Molecule takes up shape to minimise repulsions.

Water (H_2O — Figure 37)

H   Electronic configuration $1s^1$ [1]

O   Electronic configuration $1s^2\, 2s^2\, 2p^4$ [2, 6]

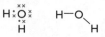

Figure 37 Water: bond angle is 104.5°; shape is bent

Explanation of shape:
- Electron pairs repel each other.
- Two bonding pairs of electrons and two lone pairs of electrons.
- Lone pairs of electrons have a greater repulsion.
- Molecule takes up shape to minimise repulsions.

Examples involving coordinate bonds

When a coordinate bond forms it converts a lone pair of electrons into a bonding pair of electrons (Figure 38). This conversion causes a change in the shape of the species formed.

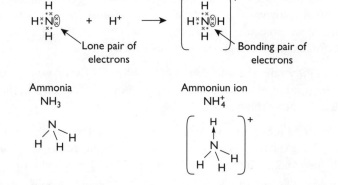

Figure 38 In ammonia the bond angle is 107° and the shape is pyramidal. In the ammonium ion the bond angle is 109.5° and the shape is tetrahedral

Explanation of shape of the ammonium ion:
- Electron pairs repel each other.
- Four bonding pairs of electrons repel each other equally.
- Molecule takes up shape to minimise repulsions.

Remember that ammonia (NH_3) is pyramidal (three bonding pairs of electrons and one lone pair of electrons), but an ammonium ion is tetrahedral (*four* bonding pairs of electrons).

Knowledge check 16

State the shape of, and bond angle in, ammonia, NH_3.

Total number of electron pairs around central atom	Number of bonding pairs of electrons	Number of lone pairs of electrons	Shape	Bond angle	Examples
2	2	0	Linear	180°	$BeCl_2$
3	3	0	Trigonal planar	120°	BF_3
4	4	0	Tetrahedral	109.5°	CH_4, NH_4^+
4	3	1	Pyramidal	107°	NH_3
4	2	2	Bent	104.5°	H_2O
6	6	0	Octahedral	90°	SF_6

Summary

Intermolecular forces

Intermolecular forces are the bonds that exist between neighbouring simple covalent molecules. There are three types of intermolecular force.

Van der Waals forces are attractions between induced dipoles (temporary dipoles caused by random movement of electrons around atoms). Van der Waals forces exist between all simple molecules and atoms in the liquid and solid states. Remember there are no forces of attraction between molecules in a gas.

Van der Waals forces are the only forces of attraction between non-polar molecules such as iodine (I_2), bromine (Br_2), sulfur (S_8), carbon dioxide (CO_2) in the solid state and liquid tetrachloromethane (CCl_4).

The more electrons present in a molecule, the greater the van der Waals forces of attraction — this explains the increase in boiling point as the chain increases in length in alkanes and the increase the boiling point on going down Group VII. Often RFM is used as a measure of the number of electrons in a molecule. Molecules with similar RFMs have comparable van der Waals forces of attraction.

Permanent dipole attractions

When a simple covalent molecule is polar, it is said to have a **permanent dipole**. The forces of attraction between polar molecules are van der Waals forces *and* permanent dipole attractions.

Permanent dipole attractions exist between polar molecules like propanone (CH_3COCH_3) and trichloromethane ($CHCl_3$) — see Figure 39.

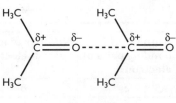

Figure 39

The permanent dipole attraction is the attraction between the $\delta+$ on one molecule and the $\delta-$ on another molecule. It is important to label the polarities ($\delta+$ and $\delta-$) of the polar bonds involved.

Hydrogen bonds (H bonds) are intermolecular forces where the bond is formed between a $\delta+$ H atom bonded to N, O or F with a $\delta-$ of a polar bond of another molecule. The hydrogen bond is formed because of the attraction between a lone pair of electrons on the $\delta-$ atom and the $\delta+$ hydrogen atom (Figure 40).

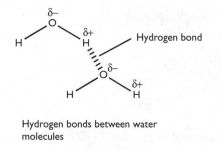

Hydrogen bonds between water molecules

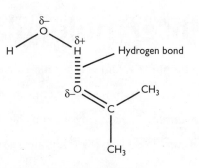

Hydrogen bonds between water and propanone molecules

Figure 40

Hydrogen bonds are often shown as dashed lines between the H (bonded to N, O or F) and the δ− atom on another molecule.

Explanation of properties using intermolecular forces

Intermolecular forces are used to explain a physical property — for example, melting point or boiling point — of a simple covalent substance. For example, 'a large amount of energy is needed to break the [intermolecular force(s) — state which one(s)] between the molecules'.

They are also used when explaining viscosity which is the opposite of fluidity (the more viscous a liquid the less well it flows). For example, 'the greater the [intermolecular force(s) — state which one(s)] between the molecules, the greater the viscosity'.

Liquids can be described as miscible (able to mix together in all proportions, forming one layer) or immiscible (unable to mix together and forming two distinct layers). Liquids often mix with each because of their ability to form the same intermolecular forces between the molecules. Solids are soluble in a solvent because they have similar bonds between their molecules.

Example: Explain why water has a higher than expected boiling point.

Answer: A large amount of energy is needed to break the hydrogen bonds between water molecules.

Example: Explain why iodine has a higher boiling point than bromine.

Answer: I_2 has more electrons than Br_2, so there are more van der Waals forces of attraction between the molecules of I_2.

Example: Explain why the liquid alkanes increase in viscosity as the carbon chain increases in length.

Answer: The number of electrons increases as the carbon chain length increases so van der Waals forces are stronger between molecules, making the alkane less fluid in the liquid state.

Example: Explain why ethanol mixes with water.

Answer: Ethanol has OH groups that can form hydrogen bonds with water molecules.

Example: Explain why bromine mixes with hexane.

Answer: Bromine and hexane are both non-polar and like dissolves like.

Example: Explain why sodium chloride dissolves in water.

Answer: Sodium chloride is an ionic substance and water is polar — like dissolves like.

Hydrides of Groups IV, V, VI and VII

Figure 41 shows the boiling points of the hydrides of Groups IV, V, VI and VII.

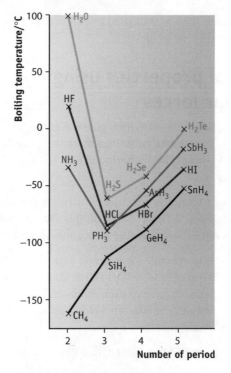

Figure 41

The boiling points of H_2O, HF and NH_3 are higher than expected. This is because of hydrogen bonds between the molecules of these compounds. CH_4 does not form hydrogen bonds between its molecules as it is non-polar.

Note in Figure 41 the increase in boiling point from H_2S to H_2Te (and the same in the other groups). This increase is due to the higher number of electrons in the molecules, which increases the van der Waals forces of attraction between the molecules.

Ice

Ice has a lower density than liquid water, so ice floats. This is because the hydrogen bonds in ice are more ordered (fixed) and the water molecules in ice are further apart, leading to a more open structure and so a lower density.

- Intermolecular forces exist between simple molecules.
- Simple molecules can be molecules of elements or compounds.
- The three forces of attraction between simple molecules are van der Waals forces of attraction, permanent dipole attractions and hydrogen bonds.
- Non-polar molecules and simple atoms (like the noble gases) have only van der Waals forces of attraction between their particles in the solid and liquid states.
- Van der Waals forces of attraction are caused by induced dipoles, which are the result of the random movement of electrons.

- The greater the number of electrons in a molecule (or atom), the greater the van der Waals forces of attraction.
- Polar molecules have permanent dipole attractions between the molecules, as well as van der Waals forces of attraction.
- In certain cases where an H atom bonded to an N, O or F atom is bonded to an electronegative atom, this is called a hydrogen bond.
- Hydrogen bonds are the strongest of the intermolecular forces of attraction.
- Physical properties of simple covalent elements or compounds can be explained in terms of the intermolecular forces between their molecules.

Redox

Redox is oxidation and reduction occurring simultaneously in the same reaction. There are four different definitions of both oxidation and reduction:

- Oxidation is:
  - loss of electrons
  - gain of oxygen
  - loss of hydrogen
  - increase in oxidation number
- Reduction is:
  - gain of electrons
  - loss of oxygen
  - gain of hydrogen
  - decrease in oxidation number

Oxidation number is the charge on a simple ion or the difference in the number of electrons associated with an atom in a compound compared with the atoms of the element.

Working with oxidation numbers

There are rules for working with oxidation numbers.

(1) The oxidation number of the atoms in an element is 0 (zero). For example:
  - the oxidation number of Na atoms in sodium metal is 0
  - the oxidation number of both Cl atoms in Cl_2 is 0
  - the oxidation number of all eight S atoms in S_8 is 0

(2) Oxidation numbers are always written as positive or negative integers (whole numbers), for example +2, –1, +7.

(3) Fractional oxidation numbers are possible but only as the average of several atoms in a compound, for example in Fe_3O_4 the oxidation number of iron is $+2\frac{2}{3}$ as two of the iron atoms have an oxidation number of +3 and one has an oxidation number of +2 — the average is $+2\frac{2}{3}$.

The **oxidation number** of a particular atom in a compound or ion is a measure of the number of electrons lost, gained or shared.

(4) Oxygen has an oxidation number of −2 in almost all compounds except in peroxides (e.g. H_2O_2, where it is −1) and in the compound F_2O, where it is +2 (fluorine is more electronegative).

(5) Hydrogen has an oxidation number of +1 in almost all compounds except hydrides, for example NaH, where it is −1.

(6) Group I elements have an oxidation number of +1 in all compounds.

(7) Group II elements have an oxidation number of +2 in all compounds.

(8) The oxidation number of ions in a compound is equal to the charge on the ion. For example:
  – in iron(II) chloride, iron has an oxidation number of +2
  – in copper(II) sulfate, copper has an oxidation number of +2
  – in silver(I) nitrate, silver has an oxidation number of +1
  – in sodium chloride, chlorine has an oxidation number of −1
  – in magnesium oxide, oxygen has an oxidation number of −2

(9) The total of the oxidation numbers for the atoms in a compound must equal 0 (zero).

(10) The total of the oxidation numbers of the atoms in a molecular ion must equal the charge on the ion. For example:
  – the total of the oxidation numbers of the atoms of the elements in sulfate, SO_4^{2-}, must equal −2
  – the total of the oxidation numbers of the atoms of the elements in nitrate, NO_3^-, must equal −1

(11) The oxidation numbers of the p and d block elements vary significantly.

(12) The maximum oxidation number of a p block element is '+ group number'. For example:
  – the maximum oxidation number of Cl is +7
  – the maximum oxidation number of N is +5

(13) The minimum oxidation number of a p block element is 'group number − 8'. For example:
  – the minimum oxidation number of Cl = 7 − 8 = −1
  – the minimum oxidation number of N = 5 − 8 = −3

(14) The d block elements can vary up to +7.

Calculating oxidation number

The above rules for working with oxidation numbers are used to calculate oxidation numbers of different atoms in compounds and ions.

Worked example 1

Determine the oxidation number of S in sodium sulfate, Na_2SO_4.

Na   oxidation number = +1; two Na atoms present, so total for Na = +2

S   oxidation number = x (the unknown)

O   oxidation number = −2; four O atoms present, so total for O = −8

Na_2SO_4 $+2 + x − 8 = 0$ (total of oxidation number is zero, as it is a compound)

$x = +8 − 2 = +6$

Oxidation number of S in Na_2SO_4 is +6

Worked example 2

Determine the oxidation number of Mn in potassium permanganate, $KMnO_4$

K   oxidation number = +1

Mn   oxidation number = x

O   oxidation number = –2; four O atoms present, so total = –8

$KMnO_4$ +1 + x – 8 = 0 (total of oxidation number is zero as it is a compound)

x = +8 – 1 = +7

Oxidation number of Mn in $KMnO_4$ = +7

Worked example 3

Determine the oxidation number of Cr in the dichromate ion, $Cr_2O_7{}^{2-}$.

Cr   oxidation number = x; two Cr atoms present, so $2x$

O   oxidation number = –2; seven O atoms present, so total = –14

Cr_2O_7 $2x$ – 14 = –2 (total of oxidation number is –2 as it is an ion)

$2x$ = –2 + 14 = +12 x = +6

Oxidation number of each Cr atom in $Cr_2O_7{}^{2-}$ is +6

Knowledge check 19

What is the oxidation number of nitrogen in nitrate, $NO_3{}^-$?

Explaining redox

Remember it is often d block and p block elements that are oxidised and reduced, but watch out for elements from other groups oxidised from/reduced to zero oxidation number.

When given a redox equation and asked to explain why it is described as redox, you need to calculate the oxidation numbers of the elements that are oxidised or reduced (Figure 42).

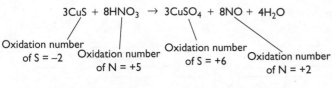

$$3CuS + 8HNO_3 \rightarrow 3CuSO_4 + 8NO + 4H_2O$$

Oxidation number of S = –2

Oxidation number of N = +5

Oxidation number of S = +6

Oxidation number of N = +2

- Sulfur is oxidised from –2 to +6
- Nitrogen is reduced from +5 to +2
- Redox is where oxidation and reduction occur in the same reaction

Figure 42

Proper names for compounds

In sodium sulfate the oxidation number of the sulfur is +6, so the proper name for sodium sulfate is sodium sulfate(VI). The VI represents the oxidation number of the S in sulfate.

In the dichromate ion, $Cr_2O_7{}^{2-}$, the oxidation number of both chromium atoms is +6, so the proper name for the dichromate ion is dichromate(VI).

Half-equations

A half-equation is an oxidation or reduction equation involving loss or gain of electrons. Examples of simple half-equations are:

$$Mg \rightarrow Mg^{2+} + 2e^-$$

This is an oxidation as 1 mol of magnesium atoms loses 2 mol of electrons to form 1 mol of magnesium ions.

$$Cl_2 + 2e^- \rightarrow 2Cl^-$$

This is a reduction as 1 mol of chlorine molecules gains 2 mol of electrons to form 2 mol of chloride ions.

$$Fe^{2+} \rightarrow Fe^{3+} + e^-$$

This is an oxidation as 1 mol of iron(II) ions loses 1 mol of electrons to form 1 mol of iron(III) ions.

NB: If the equation is oxidation, the electrons are on the right-hand side. If the equation is reduction the electrons are on the left-hand side.

More complex half-equations involve calculation of oxidation numbers and balancing any oxygen atoms gained or lost using H^+ ions and water.

Worked examples

Manganate(VII), MnO_4^- can be reduced to manganese(II), Mn^{2+}

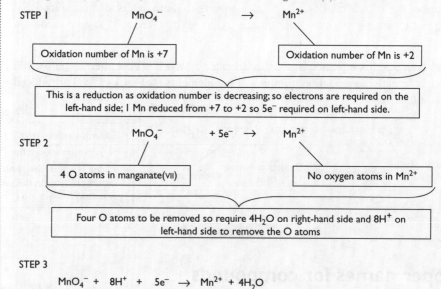

Examiner tip

The overall charge on the left and on the right of any half-equation or ionic equation should be the same if the equation is balanced correctly. Check that the overall charges on both sides match to make sure that the half-equation is correct.

Left total charge = −1 + 8 − 5 = +2
Right total charge = +2

STEP 1 MnO_4^- $\rightarrow$ Mn^{2+}

Oxidation number of Mn is +7   Oxidation number of Mn is +2

This is a reduction as oxidation number is decreasing; so electrons are required on the left-hand side; 1 Mn reduced from +7 to +2 so 5e⁻ required on left-hand side.

STEP 2 MnO_4^- $+ 5e^-$ $\rightarrow$ Mn^{2+}

4 O atoms in manganate(VII)   No oxygen atoms in Mn^{2+}

Four O atoms to be removed so require $4H_2O$ on right-hand side and $8H^+$ on left-hand side to remove the O atoms

STEP 3

$$MnO_4^- + 8H^+ + 5e^- \rightarrow Mn^{2+} + 4H_2O$$

Figure 43

Dichromate(VI), $Cr_2O_7^{2-}$ can be reduced to chromium(III), Cr^{3+}

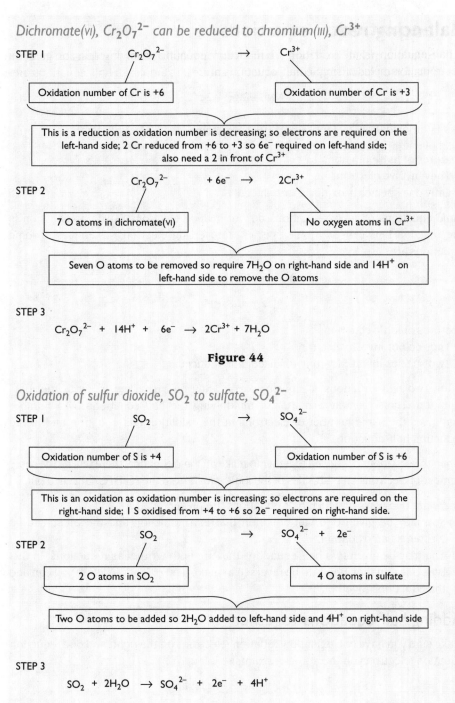

Figure 44

Oxidation of sulfur dioxide, SO_2 to sulfate, SO_4^{2-}

STEP 1

$SO_2 \rightarrow SO_4^{2-}$

Oxidation number of S is +4

Oxidation number of S is +6

This is an oxidation as oxidation number is increasing; so electrons are required on the right-hand side; 1 S oxidised from +4 to +6 so 2e⁻ required on right-hand side.

STEP 2

$SO_2 \rightarrow SO_4^{2-} + 2e^-$

2 O atoms in SO_2

4 O atoms in sulfate

Two O atoms to be added so $2H_2O$ added to left-hand side and $4H^+$ on right-hand side

STEP 3

$SO_2 + 2H_2O \rightarrow SO_4^{2-} + 2e^- + 4H^+$

Figure 45

Knowledge check 20

Write a half-equation for the reduction of sulfate(IV) ions (SO_3^{2-}) to sulfur.

Balancing redox equations

Half-equations include electrons. A half-equation is half a redox reaction and involves the oxidation or reduction of one particular species. Examples of half-equations are:

$$Ni \rightarrow Ni^{2+} + 2e^-$$

$$Cr_2O_7^{2-} + 14H^+ + 6e^- \rightarrow 2Cr^{3+} + 7H_2O$$

Features of half-equations:
- They involve electrons.
- Only one species is oxidised or reduced.

Ionic equations or redox equations do not include electrons. An ionic equation is the reaction between two ionic species transferring electrons. Examples of ionic equations are:

$$Mg + 2H^+ \rightarrow Mg^{2+} + H_2$$

$$Cl_2 + 2I^- \rightarrow 2Cl^- + I_2$$

Features of ionic equations:
- They do not involve electrons.
- Two species involved — one oxidised, one reduced.

Often two half-equations are given to you and you are asked to write the ionic equation. This is simply a matter of multiplying the half-equations by a number that gives the same number of electrons in the oxidation half-equation and in the reduction half-equation.

When the equations are added together to make an ionic equation, there will be the same number of electrons on both sides of the ionic equation so they can be cancelled out.

There are two ways in which half-equations are presented at AS and A2:
(1) You may be given one half-equation that is a reduction and the other will be written as an oxidation.
(2) You may be given two half-equations that are both written as reductions. In this type one equation needs to be reversed to make it an oxidation before you can add the equations together.

Adding half-equations together

Make sure you have one oxidation equation (electrons on the right) and one reduction equation (electrons on the left). For example:

$$Al \rightarrow Al^{3+} + 3e^- \qquad \text{Oxidation}$$

$$F_2 + 2e^- \rightarrow 2F^- \qquad \text{Reduction}$$

Make sure the numbers of electrons are the same in both the oxidation and reduction half-equations. To do this the oxidation equation needs to be multiplied by 2. The reduction equation needs to be multiplied by 3. This will give both equations 6 electrons:

$$2Al \rightarrow 2Al^{3+} + 6e^-$$

$$3F_2 + 6e^- \rightarrow 6F^-$$

To add them, simply write down all the species from the left-hand side of both half-equations, then put an arrow and finally write down all the species from the right-hand side of both half-equations:

$$2Al + 3F_2 + 6e^- \rightarrow 2Al^{3+} + 6e^- + 6F^-$$

The next step is to cancel out the electrons on both sides of the ionic equation:

$$2Al + 3F_2 \rightarrow 2Al^{3+} + 6F^-$$

This is the ionic equation for the reaction between aluminium and fluorine.

Examiner tip

Always check an ionic equation for charges on the left-hand side and right-hand side; the total charges should be the same on both sides: 0 on the left-hand side and 0 on the right-hand side.

Worked example I

Iron(II) ions are oxidised by acidified potassium manganate(VII).

The two half-equations are:

Oxidation $\quad\quad$ $Fe^{2+} \rightarrow Fe^{3+} + e^-$

Reduction $\quad\quad$ $MnO_4^- + 8H^+ + 5e^- \rightarrow Mn^{2+} + 4H_2O$

There are five electrons on the left-hand side of the second equation and only one electron on the right-hand side of the first equation.

In order to write a complete ionic equation, the first equation must be multiplied by 5 and then the two equations are simply added together.

$$5Fe^{2+} \rightarrow 5Fe^{3+} + 5e^-$$

$$MnO_4^- + 8H^+ + 5e^- \rightarrow Mn^{2+} + 4H_2O$$
_____

$$MnO_4^- + 8H^+ + 5e^- + 5Fe^{2+} \rightarrow Mn^{2+} + 4H_2O + 5Fe^{3+} + 5e^-$$

The $5e^-$ on each side can be cancelled so that the overall equation reads:

$$MnO_4^- + 8H^+ + 5Fe^{2+} \rightarrow Mn^{2+} + 4H_2O + 5Fe^{3+}$$

Sometimes the half-equations are given as two reductions, so one equation must be reversed to enable the electrons to be eliminated. The reaction will indicate which two species are reacting. The following could be the way in which the above example was presented:

Reduction $\quad\quad$ $Fe^{3+} + e^- \rightarrow Fe^{2+}$

Reduction $\quad\quad$ $MnO_4^- + 8H^+ + 5e^- \rightarrow Mn^{2+} + 4H_2O$

You are asked to write an ionic equation for the reaction between iron(II) ions, Fe^{2+}, and manganate(VII) ions, MnO_4-. The reaction requires the first half-equation to be reversed to $Fe^{2+} \rightarrow Fe^{3+} + e^-$ and then multiplied by 5 as before.

The final equation is the same when the electrons have been eliminated.

$$MnO_4^- + 8H^+ + 5Fe^{2+} \rightarrow Mn^{2+} + 4H_2O + 5Fe^{3+}$$

Worked example 2

Write an ionic equation for the reaction of nitrate(III) ions, NO_2^- and dichromate(VI) ions, $Cr_2O_7^{2-}$ using the following half-equations:

$$NO_2^- + H_2O \rightarrow NO_3^- + 2H^+ + 2e^-$$

$$Cr_2O_7^{2-} + 14H^+ + 6e^- \rightarrow 2Cr^{3+} + 7H_2O$$

The equations given are an oxidation (first equation) and a reduction (second equation) so they can be combined directly once the electrons have been balanced:

$$3NO_2^- + 3H_2O \rightarrow 3NO_3^- + 6H^+ + 6e^-$$

$$Cr_2O_7^{2-} + 14H^+ + 6e^- \rightarrow 2Cr^{3+} + 7H_2O$$

$$\overline{Cr_2O_7^{2-} + 14H^+ + 3NO_2^- + 3H_2O + 6e^- \rightarrow 2Cr^{3+} + 7H_2O + 3NO_3^- + 6H^+ + 6e^-}$$

The electrons, water and H^+ need to be cancelled:

$$Cr_2O_7^{2-} + 8H^+ + 3NO_2^- \rightarrow 2Cr^{3+} + 4H_2O + 3NO_3^-$$

Disproportionation

A disproportionation reaction is one in which the same element is oxidised and reduced in the same reaction (Figure 46).

$$H_2O + Cl_2 \rightarrow HOCl + HCl$$

Oxidation number of $Cl = 0$

Oxidation number of $Cl = +1$

Oxidation number of $Cl = -1$

- Chlorine is oxidised from 0 to +1
- Chlorine is reduced from 0 to −1
- Chlorine is oxidised and reduced in the same reaction = disproportionation

Figure 46

Knowledge check 21

What is meant by the term disproportionation?

Summary

- The oxidation number (or oxidation state) of a particular atom in a compound or ion is a measure of the number of electrons lost, gained or shared.
- Hydrogen has an oxidation number of +1 in almost all compounds and ions except hydrides.
- Oxygen has an oxidation number of −2 in almost all compounds and ions except peroxides.
- In a compound, Group I atoms have an oxidation number of +1; Group II atoms +2; and Al +3.
- Transition atoms in compounds and ions vary in their oxidation number.
- Non-zero oxidation numbers should always be stated with a + or − sign.
- The total oxidation number in a compound equals zero.
- The total oxidation number in a molecular ion equals the charge on the ion.
- Half-equations represent oxidation and reduction; reduction is gain of electrons and oxidation is loss of electrons.
- When combining half-equations the number of electrons are made to cancel out and any H^+ ions and H_2O can cancel down.

The Periodic Table and Group VII

The Periodic Table lists all known elements in order of atomic number. The atomic number is the same as the number of protons in the nucleus of atoms and ions of the element. The elements are arranged in groups and periods with distinct blocks.

The columns in the Periodic Table are called groups and the rows are called periods.
- Group I: Li, Na, K etc.   Period 1: H and He
- Group II: Mg, Ca, etc.   Period 2: Li to Ne
- Group VII: F, Cl, Br, I, etc.   Period 3: Na to Ar
- Group 0: He, Ne, Ar, Kr etc.   Period 4: K to Kr

Group names:
- Group I: alkali metals (a group of reactive metals)
- Group II: alkaline earth metals (a group of reactive metals)
- Group VII: halogens (a group of reactive non-metals)
- Group 0: noble gases (a group of unreactive non-metals)

The blocks of the Periodic Table are shown in Figure 11 on page 29.

The electronic configuration of atoms of elements in the same group all have the same outer shell configuration (Table 12).

Table 12

Group	Outer shell electronic configuration
I	s^1
II	s^2
III	p^1
IV	p^2
V	p^3
VI	p^4
VII	p^5
VIII	p^6

Trends in reactivity:
- Going down Group I and II, reactivity increases.
- Going down Group VII, reactivity decreases.

Periodic trends

From sodium to argon

(1) Melting point increases to Si and then decreases.
From Na to Mg to Al the metallic bond increases in strength as there are more outer shell electrons that can be delocalised, giving a greater attraction between the electrons and the ions in the metallic structure.

Silicon has a giant covalent structure and so has the highest melting point in the period as a substantial amount of energy is required to break the large number of strong covalent bonds.

Phosphorus, P_4, sulfur, S_8 and chlorine, Cl_2 are non-polar simple covalent molecules with low melting points. S_8 has the most electrons and so the greatest van der Waals forces of attraction between molecules. Argon is monatomic.

(2) Conductivity increases to aluminium and then decreases.

The three metals conduct electricity and the conduction increases from Na to Al as there are more delocalised electrons that can move and carry the charge.

(3) First ionisation energy generally increases, with Mg, P and Ar higher than expected.

Across the period the nuclear charge increases and atomic radius decreases; Group II, V and VIII first ionisation energies are higher than expected due to the stability of filled and half-filled subshells.

(4) Atomic radius decreases.

Across the period the nuclear charge increases, which pulls the outer electrons closer to the nucleus.

Group VII — the halogens

Physical properties

Physical properties of the halogens are given in Table 13.

Table 13 Physical properties of the halogens

Halogen / Property	Fluorine	Chlorine	Bromine	Iodine
Colour and physical state at room temperature	Yellow gas	Yellow-green gas	Red-brown liquid (red-brown vapour when heated)	Grey-black solid (purple vapour when heated)
Melting point (°C)	−220	−101	−7	114
Boiling point (°C)	−188	−34	59	184
Atomic radius (nm)	0.057	0.1	0.115	0.140
First ionisation energy (kJ mol⁻¹)	1681	1251	1140	1008
X_2 bond enthalpy (kJ mol⁻¹)	158	242	193	151
HX bond enthalpy (kJ mol⁻¹)	485	431	366	299
Electronegativity	4.0	3.0	2.8	2.5

The decrease in the covalent bond enthalpy values is due to the increasing atomic size of the halogen atoms. A covalent bond length is the distance from one nucleus to the other in the covalent bond. With larger atoms the bonds become longer, and longer bonds are weaker bonds. The covalent bond in F_2 does not fit the pattern as it is such a short bond that the lone pairs of electrons on each fluorine atom repel each other, weakening the bond.

Knowledge check 23

State and explain the trend in first ionisation energy across the third period from Na to Ar.

Examiner tip

You need to be able to explain the physical properties of the halogens using your knowledge of previous sections. For example, the increase in melting point, boiling point and the change in physical state can be explained in terms of van der Waals forces; the increasing atomic radius, decreasing first ionisation energy and electronegativity in terms of the outer electrons being further from the nucleus.

Bond enthalpy is the energy required to break one mole of a covalent bond. It is measured in kJ mol⁻¹.

Solubility of halogens

The halogens are non-polar simple covalent molecules. The solubility of the halogens in water (a polar solvent) decreases down the group until iodine, which is virtually insoluble in water. A solution of chlorine in water is called 'chlorine water' and a solution of bromine in water is called 'bromine water'.

All of the halogens dissolve in non-polar solvents such as hexane. (See Table 14.)

Table 14 Solubility of the halogens in water and hexane

Halogen	Solubility in water	Solubility in hexane
Chlorine	Soluble, forming a pale green/colourless solution	Soluble, forming a colourless solution
Bromine	Soluble, forming a yellow/orange/brown solution	Soluble, forming a red solution
Iodine	Virtually insoluble, but any solution formed is yellow/brown (Iodine is soluble in a solution containing iodide ions to form a brown solution; it is soluble in other polar solvents, such as ethanol, to form a yellow/brown solution)	Soluble, forming a purple solution

Reactivity of halogens

The halogens are usually represented as X_2, where X represents any halogen atom. The reactivity of the halogens decreases down the group.

Halogens reacting with hydrogen

All reactions can be represented as:

$$H_2 + X_2 \rightarrow 2HX$$

These reactions require initiation, using light – a piece of burning magnesium can be used. The reactions of hydrogen with chlorine and fluorine are explosive; the reaction of hydrogen with iodine is slow.

Observations: Misty fumes of the hydrogen halide, HX, are formed.

Halogens reacting with sodium

All reactions can be represented as:

$$2Na + X_2 \rightarrow 2NaX$$

All sodium halides, NaX, are white solids, for example NaCl, NaBr and NaI.

Halogens reacting with phosphorus

F_2, Cl_2 and Br_2 form PX_3 and then PX_5 if the halogen is present in excess. I_2 forms only PI_3, even with excess I_2.

The halogens are oxidising agents and their oxidising ability decreases down the group. F_2, Cl_2 and Br_2 are able to oxidise phosphorus from 0 to +5 oxidation numbers, but I_2 can only oxidise phosphorus from 0 to +3.

PF_3 is a colourless gas; PCl_3 and PBr_3 are colourless liquids; PI_3 is a red solid.

Knowledge check 24

Give the colours and state of iodine at room temperature and when heated.

PF_5 is a colourless gas; PCl_5 is an off-white solid; PBr_5 is a yellow solid.

During preparation from phosphorus and the halogen, water/moisture must be excluded as all phosphorus halides hydrolyse, forming various oxyacids and hydrogen halides.

Other reactions of the halogens

In these reactions chlorine is used as it is the most common example but other halogens can be substituted. Where other halogens do not react, this is made clear.

Halogens with water

$$Cl_2 + H_2O \rightarrow HOCl + HCl$$

This is an example of disproportionation where one element is oxidised and reduced in the same reaction. Chlorine is oxidised from 0 to +1 and reduced from 0 to −1.

Halogens with cold dilute alkali, e.g. NaOH(aq)

$$2NaOH + Cl_2 \rightarrow NaCl + NaClO + H_2O$$

The general ionic equation for this reaction is:

$$2OH^- + Cl_2 \rightarrow Cl^- + ClO^- + H_2O$$

NaClO is called sodium hypochlorite or sodium chlorate(I) as it contains the chlorate(I) ion, ClO^-. The oxidation number of chlorine in chlorate(I) is +1.

Halogens with hot concentrated alkali, e.g. NaOH(aq)

$$3Cl_2 + 6NaOH \rightarrow 5NaCl + NaClO_3 + 3H_2O$$

The general ionic equation for this reaction is:

$$6OH^- + 3Cl_2 \rightarrow 5Cl^- + ClO_3^- + 3H_2O$$

$NaClO_3$ is sodium chlorate(v) or simply 'sodium chlorate'. It contains the chlorate(v) ion, ClO_3^-. The oxidation number of chlorine in chlorate(v) is +5.

Iodine does not react with cold dilute alkali but will react with hot concentrated alkali to form an iodate(v), IO_3^- compound.

Again in these reactions chlorine undergoes disproportionation as it is both oxidised and reduced: Cl_2 (oxidation number = 0); Cl in Cl^- (oxidation number = −1); Cl in ClO_3^- (oxidation number = +5).

In all of the above reactions, the yellow-green gas dissolves to form a colourless solution.

Halogens with other halides in solution

A more reactive halogen will displace a less reactive one from a solution of its halide ions.

$$Cl_2 + 2Br^- \rightarrow 2Cl^- + Br_2$$

The yellow-green gas dissolves and the solution changes from colourless to orange.

$$Cl_2 + 2I^- \rightarrow 2Cl^- + I_2$$

The yellow-green gas dissolves and the solution changes from colourless to brown.

$$Br_2 + 2I^- \rightarrow 2Br^- + I_2$$

The solution changes from yellow-orange to brown.

Halogens with iron

With fluorine, chlorine and bromine, iron is oxidised to the +3 oxidation state. With iodine, iron is oxidised to only the +2 oxidation state.

$$2Fe + 3Cl_2 \rightarrow 2FeCl_3$$

$$2Fe + 3Br_2 \rightarrow 2FeBr_3$$

$$Fe + I_2 \rightarrow FeI_2$$

Halogens with iron(II) ions in solution

Fluorine, chlorine and bromine will oxidise iron(II) ions in solution to iron(III) ions.

$$2Fe^{2+} + Cl_2 \rightarrow 2Fe^{3+} + 2Cl^-$$

The colour of the solution changes from pale green $Fe^{2+}(aq)$ to yellow/orange $Fe^{3+}(aq)$.

Iodine will not oxidise iron(II) ions.

Hydrogen halides

Bond strength:
- H–F bond is the shortest and strongest.
- H–I bond is the longest and weakest.

Thermal stability:
- HF is very stable to heat.
- HCl is stable up to 1523°C.
- HBr is stable up to 800°C.
- HI is stable up to 177°C (NB: purple fumes of I_2 on heating).

Acid strength:
- For equimolar solutions of HI, HBr, HCl and HF, acid strength decreases from HI to HF. A solution of HI would have the lowest pH.
- HI has the weakest hydrogen–halogen bond, so a solution of HI would release more H^+ ions than equimolar solutions of HBr, HCl and HF.
- A solution of HF releases fewer H^+ ions than equimolar solutions of all the other hydrogen halides, as the HF bond is the strongest of the hydrogen–halogen bonds..

Test for halide ions

To test a compound for the presence of a halide ion, make a *solution* of the compound using dilute nitric acid or, if you are testing a solution for the presence of a halide ion, add a few cm^3 of dilute nitric acid to it. Then add silver nitrate solution, $AgNO_3(aq)$. A precipitate (ppt) will form if chloride, bromide or iodide ions are present. The colour of the ppt gives the identity of the ions, but dilute ammonia solution and/or concentrated ammonia solution can be used to confirm the identity of the ion present as some of the precipitates will redissolve. The dilute nitric acid removes any carbonate ions as silver carbonate is a white solid, so would give a false positive for a chloride ion.

$$2Ag^+ + CO_3^{2-} \rightarrow Ag_2CO_3$$

Examiner tip

Iodide ions in solution will reduce iron(III), Fe^{3+} to iron(II), Fe^{2+}. The iodide is oxidised to iodine. The solution will change colour from yellow/orange to brown. The ionic equation is $2Fe^{3+} + 2I^- \rightarrow 2Fe^{2+} + I_2$. Chloride and bromide ions will not reduce iron(III) to iron(II).

Examiner tip

Recalling and explaining the relative strength of equimolar solutions of the hydrogen halides and the trend in thermal stability are common questions. These are all explained in terms of the strength of the hydrogen–halogen covalent bond.

Examiner tip

When describing how to carry out a test for an ion using solutions, make sure you use the word 'solution' when needed. You will lose marks if you simply say 'add silver nitrate' or 'add dilute ammonia'. The only time 'solution' is not needed is with an acid such as dilute nitric acid. Also, remember that the silver nitrate solution needs to be added to a solution containing the ion.

- A white ppt that is soluble in dilute ammonia solution indicates the presence of chloride ions.

  Ionic equation: $Ag^+(aq) + Cl^-(aq) \rightarrow AgCl(s)$

- A cream ppt that is insoluble in dilute ammonia solution and soluble in concentrated ammonia solution indicates the presence of bromide ions.

  Ionic equation: $Ag^+(aq) + Br^-(aq) \rightarrow AgBr(s)$

- A yellow ppt that is insoluble in both dilute and concentrated ammonia solution indicates the presence of iodide ions.

  Ionic equation: $Ag^+(aq) + I^-(aq) \rightarrow AgI(s)$

The white ppt is silver chloride, AgCl; the cream ppt is silver bromide, AgBr; and the yellow ppt is silver iodide, AgI.

Halides and concentrated sulfuric acid

Solid halide compounds react with concentrated sulfuric acid. The equations, observations and names of the products of these reactions are common questions.

Chloride with concentrated sulfuric acid

Equation:

$$NaCl + H_2SO_4 \rightarrow NaHSO_4 + HCl$$

This is not a redox equation; HCl has no reducing ability. HSO_4^- is the hydrogen-sulfate ion.

Observations: misty fumes (HCl); heat released; gas produced; solid disappears; pungent smell (HCl)

Names of products: sodium hydrogensulfate and hydrogen chloride

The reaction with a solid fluoride is similar to that of the chloride, releasing misty fumes of hydrogen fluoride, but is too dangerous to be carried out in a school laboratory.

Bromide with concentrated sulfuric acid

Equations:

$$NaBr + H_2SO_4 \rightarrow NaHSO_4 + HBr$$

$$2HBr + H_2SO_4 \rightarrow Br_2 + SO_2 + 2H_2O$$

HBr has some reducing ability so H_2SO_4 is reduced to SO_2 and bromide is oxidised to Br_2.

Observations: misty fumes (HBr); heat released; gas produced; solid disappears; red-brown vapour (Br_2); pungent smell (HBr/SO_2/Br_2)

Names of products: sodium hydrogensulfate, hydrogen bromide, bromine, sulfur dioxide and water

Iodide with concentrated sulfuric acid

Equations:

$$NaI + H_2SO_4 \rightarrow NaHSO_4 + HI$$

$$2HI + H_2SO_4 \rightarrow I_2 + SO_2 + 2H_2O$$

$$6HI + H_2SO_4 \rightarrow 3I_2 + S + 4H_2O$$

$$8HI + H_2SO_4 \rightarrow 4I_2 + H_2S + 4H_2O$$

HI has good reducing ability, so H_2SO_4 is reduced to SO_2, S and H_2S, while iodide is oxidised to I_2.

Observations: misty fumes (HI); heat released; gas produced; solid disappears; purple vapour and grey-black solid (I_2); pungent smell (HI/SO_2/I_2); rotten eggs smell (H_2S); yellow solid (S)

Names of products: sodium hydrogensulfate; hydrogen iodide; iodine; sulfur dioxide; sulfur; hydrogen sulfide; water

Fluoride in drinking water

Fluoride ions are reported to help prevent tooth decay. Sodium fluoride is added to toothpaste and in some areas it is added to drinking water. Some people campaign against fluoridation of drinking water, arguing that people should have the freedom of choice and that this is mass medication.

Examiner tip

The reactions with concentrated sulfuric can be used as an alternative test for a halide:

- Chlorides give hydrogen chloride gas with concentrated sulfuric acid, which can be tested using a glass rod dipped in concentrated ammonia solution to give white smoke.
- Bromides give bromine vapour with concentrated sulfuric acid, which can be seen as brown fumes.
- Iodides give iodine with concentrated sulfuric acid, which can be seen as purple fumes and/or a grey solid.

Knowledge check 26

Write two equations for the reactions of concentrated sulfuric acid with potassium bromide.

Summary

- The Periodic Table is made up of groups (vertical columns) and periods (horizontal rows).
- There are specific trends across a period and down particular groups.
- Group VII comprises the halogens, which are coloured, non-metallic, reactive elements.
- The halogens react directly with sodium, phosphorus, iron and some other halide ions in solution.
- Halide ions can be tested for using silver nitrate solution. The colour of the precipitate and whether it redissolves in ammonia solution indicate the halide ion present.
- Solid halide compounds (chlorides, bromides and iodides) react with concentrated sulfuric acid.
- The hydrogen–halogen bond increases in length and decreases in strength down the group and this can be used to explain thermal stability and acid strength in solution.

Titrations

A titration is a method of volumetric analysis. One solution is placed in a burette and the other is placed in a conical flask. An indicator is added to the solution in the conical flask. The solution in the burette is then added to the solution in the conical flask. The indicator will show the end point of the titration (when the indicator changes colour). This is the point when the reaction is complete.

Apparatus and practical techniques

The main pieces of apparatus used in a titration are a burette, a pipette with safety filler, a volumetric flask and several conical flasks.

Preparing a burette for use

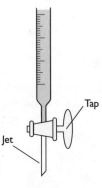

Figure 47

- Rinse the burette with deionised water.
- Ensure the water flows through the jet.
- Discard the water.
- Rinse the burette with the solution you will be filling it with.
- Ensure the solution flows through the jet.
- Discard the solution.
- Charge (fill) the burette with the solution you will be using in it, ensuring that the jet is filled.

Using a burette

When using a burette the volume of solution it contains is read at the bottom of the meniscus, as shown in Figure 48. If you are right-handed the tap of the burette is operated with the left hand to allow the right hand to be used to swirl to mix the contents of the conical flask.

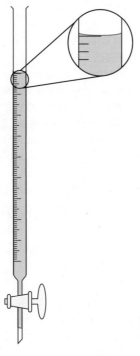

Figure 48

Preparing a pipette for use in a titration

- Using a pipette filler, rinse the pipette using deionised water.
- Discard the water.
- Rinse the pipette with the solution you will be filling it with.
- Discard this solution.

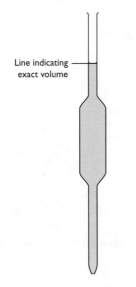

Line indicating exact volume

Figure 49 A typical pipette

Using a pipette

A pipette accurately measures an exact volume of a solution and should be used in the following way:

- A pipette filler is attached to the top of a pipette.
- The pipette is placed in the solution and suction applied to draw the solution up.
- The solution is drawn up above the line on the pipette.
- The solution is released until the meniscus sits on the line.
- The solution in the pipette is released into a conical flask.

Pipettes measure out exactly $25.0\,cm^3$ or $10.0\,cm^3$.

(Remember that $1\,cm^3 = 1\,ml$ but chemists prefer cm^3 as their volume unit.)

An exact volume of a solution is vital in volumetric work as taking $25.0\,cm^3$ of a solution of known concentration means that we know exactly how many moles of the dissolved substance are present in the conical flask.

Conical flasks

Conical flasks are used in titrations as they can be swirled easily to mix the reactants. Also the sloped sides prevent any of the solution spitting out when it is being added. The conical flask should be rinsed out with deionised water before use.

The conical flask does not have to be completely dry before use as the volume of solution added contains an exact number of moles of solute. Extra deionised water does not add to the number of moles of solute.

Volumetric flasks

Volumetric flasks (Figure 50) are used when diluting one of the solutions before the titration is carried out. They can also be used when preparing a solution of a solid.

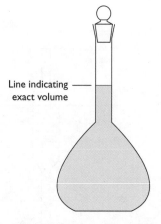

Line indicating exact volume

Figure 50 A volumetric flask

Carrying out a dilution of a solution

- Pipette $25.0\,cm^3$ of the original solution into a clean volumetric flask.
- Add deionised water to the flask until the water is just below the line.
- Using a disposable pipette add deionised water very slowly until the bottom of the meniscus is on the line.
- Stopper the flask and invert to mix thoroughly.

Dilution factor

The dilution factor is the amount the original solution is diluted by. It is calculated by dividing the new total volume by the volume of original solution put into the mixture. For example:

- If a $25.0\,cm^3$ sample of a solution is made up to a total volume of $250.0\,cm^3$ using deionised water then the dilution factor is 10.
- If a $10.0\,cm^3$ sample of a solution is made up to a total volume of $250.0\,cm^3$ using deionised water then the dilution factor is 25.

Preparing a solution from a mass of solid

When preparing a solution from a solid it is important not to lose any of the solid or solution before it is placed in the volumetric flask.

- Weigh out an accurate mass of a solid in a weighing boat and dissolve in a suitable volume of deionised water in a beaker — stirring with a glass rod — then rinse the weighing boat into the beaker with deionised water.
- Once the solid has dissolved, hold the glass rod above the beaker and rinse it with deionised water before removing it
- Place a glass funnel into the top of a clean volumetric flask and pour the prepared solution down a glass rod into the funnel.
- Rinse the glass rod with deionised water into the funnel.
- Rinse the funnel with deionised water.
- Remove the funnel and add deionised water to the volumetric flask until the water is just below the line.
- Using a disposable pipette, add deionised water very slowly until the bottom of the meniscus is on the line.
- Stopper the flask and invert to mix thoroughly.

Carrying out a titration

The major points in carrying out a titration are shown in Figure 51.

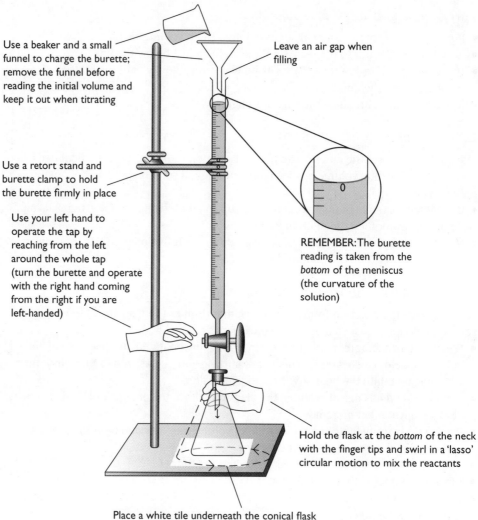

Use a beaker and a small funnel to charge the burette; remove the funnel before reading the initial volume and keep it out when titrating

Leave an air gap when filling

Use a retort stand and burette clamp to hold the burette firmly in place

Use your left hand to operate the tap by reaching from the left around the whole tap (turn the burette and operate with the right hand coming from the right if you are left-handed)

REMEMBER: The burette reading is taken from the *bottom* of the meniscus (the curvature of the solution)

Hold the flask at the *bottom* of the neck with the finger tips and swirl in a 'lasso' circular motion to mix the reactants

Place a white tile underneath the conical flask to view the indicator colour more clearly

Figure 51 Carrying out a titration

In one volumetric analysis, three titrations should be carried out:

- The first titration should be rough and should be an overshoot, but no more than $1 \, cm^3$ greater than the accurate titrations.
- The second and third titrations should be accurate, with dropwise addition as the end point is reached.

Standard solutions are used in volumetric analysis. A **standard solution** is a solution of known concentration.

A burette has a total graduated volume of $50.0 \, cm^3$. You can perform two titrations using a burette if the titres are well below $25.0 \, cm^3$. However, if the rough is close to or above $25.0 \, cm^3$, it is essential you refill the burette before starting the first accurate titration.

Recording titration results

Table 15 is a typical table used to record titration results.

Table 15

	Initial burette reading/cm^3	Final burette reading/cm^3	Titre/cm^3
Rough			
1st accurate			
2nd accurate			

The titre is the volume delivered from the burette into the conical flask until the indicator changes colour (end point). 'Volume delivered' is sometimes used in the table instead of 'titre'.

Please note the following points about recording titration results:
- You should put units with the headings and never put units in the main body of the table.
- All values should be recorded to a minimum of 1 decimal place — i.e. 0 cm^3 is written as 0.0 cm^3; 25 cm^3 is written as 25.0 cm^3.
- The rough titration titre should be greater than the two accurate titration titres but not more than 1 cm^3 greater.
- The two accurate titration titre values should be within 0.1 cm^3 of each other. Titrations should be carried out until two values within 0.1 cm^3 of each other are obtained.
- The average titre must be stated with units to a minimum of 1 decimal place. 2 decimal places are acceptable, e.g. 23.95 cm^3, if necessary. However, if the average titre is 24.0 cm^3, do not write 24.00 cm^3.

Your results are marked according to how closely grouped the two accurate titres are.

Calculating the average titre

When calculating the average titre, ignore the rough titration and any result that is clearly not within 0.1 cm^3 of the other accurate titration values.

Write the average titre below the table and include the units. The average titre can be written to two decimal places. Table 16 shows an example.

Table 16 Sample titration results table

	Initial burette reading/cm^3	Final burette reading/cm^3	Titre/cm^3
Rough	0.0	24.5	24.5
1st accurate	0.0	24.0	24.0
2nd accurate	24.0	47.9	23.9

Average titre = 23.95 cm^3

Units

- Units of volume are in cm^3 ($1\,cm^3 = 1\,ml$).
- Concentration units are mol/dm^3. This can also be written as $mol\,dm^{-3}$.
- Remember that $1\,dm^3$ is the same as 1 litre.
- However, M (molar) may also be used and is the same as $mol\,dm^{-3}$.
- A 1 M solution is $1\,mol\,dm^{-3}$. The molarity of a solution has units M but concentration is usually quoted as $mol\,dm^{-3}$ (it also can be given in $g\,dm^{-3}$).
- Concentration in g/dm^3 (grams per dm^3) can be calculated by multiplying the concentration (or molarity) by the RFM of the solute.

Common acids and bases

Strong acids: HCl, H_2SO_4, HNO_3 Weak acids: CH_3COOH, organic acids

Strong bases: $NaOH$, KOH Weak bases: NH_3, Na_2CO_3

Common equations used in titrations:

$$NaOH + HCl \rightarrow NaCl + H_2O \quad \text{1:1 ratio for NaOH:HCl}$$

$$2NaOH + H_2SO_4 \rightarrow Na_2SO_4 + 2H_2O \quad \text{2:1 ratio for NaOH:}H_2SO_4$$

$$NaOH + CH_3COOH \rightarrow CH_3COONa + H_2O \quad \text{1:1 ratio for NaOH:}CH_3COOH$$

(Each of the above can be rewritten with KOH, and the same ratio applies.)

$$Na_2CO_3 + 2HCl \rightarrow 2NaCl + CO_2 + H_2O \quad \text{1:2 ratio for Na}_2CO_3\text{:HCl}$$

$$Na_2CO_3 + H_2SO_4 \rightarrow Na_2SO_4 + CO_2 + H_2O \quad \text{1:1 ratio for Na}_2CO_3\text{:}H_2SO_4$$

The ratio between the solutes is important as it gives the ratio between the number of moles of the substance added from the burette and the number of moles of the other substance in the conical flask.

Indicators

The two main indicators used for acid–base titrations are phenolphthalein and methyl orange (Table 17).

Table 17 Features of phenolphthalein and methyl orange

Indicator	Phenolphthalein	Methyl orange
Colour in acidic solutions	Colourless	Red/pink
Colour in neutral solutions	Colourless	Orange
Colour in alkaline solutions	Pink	Yellow
Titrations suitable for	Strong acid–strong base Weak acid–strong base	Strong acid–strong base Strong acid–weak base

The colour change of the indicator at the end point is frequently asked (Table 18).

Examiner tip

The choice of indicator is based on the types of acid and base in the titration. It is important to be able to choose the correct indicator for a particular titration. If ethanoic acid (a weak acid) and sodium hydroxide solution (a strong alkali) are being used then phenolphthalein is the indicator of choice. Both methyl orange and phenolphthalein can be used for strong acid–strong base titrations.

Table 18 Colour changes of phenolphthalein and methyl orange

Titration	Phenolphthalein	Methyl orange
Acid in conical flask/ alkali in burette	Colourless to pink	Red/pink to orange/yellow
Alkali in conical flask/ acid in burette	Pink to colourless	Yellow to red/orange/pink

Typical method of acid–base titration

- The solution of known concentration is usually placed in the burette.
- Using a pipette filler, rinse a pipette with deionised water and with the solution you are going to pipette into the conical flask. Pipette 25.0 cm³ of this solution into three different conical flasks.
- Add 3–5 drops of a suitable indicator to each conical flask.
- Note the colour of the indicator in this solution.
- Rinse a burette with deionised water and with the solution you are using to fill it with. Fill the burette with this solution. Titrate until the indicator just changes colour, adding dropwise near the end point.
- Repeat for accuracy and calculate the average titre from two accurate titre values.

Volumetric calculations

Calculations involving solutions are a little more complex as you are dealing with a solution volume and a concentration of the solution to determine the number of moles of solute present. The expressions used is:

$$\text{number of moles} = \frac{\text{solution volume } (cm^3) \times \text{concentration } (mol\,dm^{-3})}{1000}$$

Typical acid–base calculation question

A solution of oven cleaner contains sodium hydroxide. 25.0 cm³ of this solution were pipetted into a 250 cm³ volumetric flask and the solution made up to the mark with deionised water. 25.0 cm³ of this solution were placed in a conical flask and titrated against 0.02 mol dm⁻³ hydrochloric acid using phenolphthalein indicator. The average titre was determined to be 17.2 cm³.

Standard types of part questions asked

(a) Calculate the number of moles of hydrochloric acid added from the burette.
(b) Write a balanced symbol equation for the reaction between sodium hydroxide and hydrochloric acid.
(c) Calculate the number of moles of sodium hydroxide present in 25.0 cm³ of the diluted solution.

From this point the calculation can go one of two ways.

Examiner tip

Make sure you know what solution is present in the conical flask and what solution is being added from the burette to determine the colour change. For example, if sodium hydroxide is being added from the burette to hydrochloric acid in the conical flask with phenolphthalein, the colour change is colourless to pink.

Knowledge check 28

State the colour change when hydrochloric acid is added to sodium hydroxide solution containing phenolphthalein.

Examiner tip

These questions are often structured and follow a pattern — the first calculation will be a number of moles of a solute from a solution volume and concentration.

(d) Calculate the concentration of the diluted sodium hydroxide solution in mol dm^{-3}
(e) Calculate the concentration of the undiluted sodium hydroxide solution in mol dm^{-3}.
(f) Calculate the concentration of the undiluted sodium hydroxide solution in g dm^{-3}.

or

(d) Calculate the number of moles of sodium hydroxide present in 250 cm^3 of the diluted solution.
(e) Calculate the number of moles of sodium hydroxide present in 25.0 cm^3 of the original solution.
(f) Calculate the concentration of the undiluted sodium hydroxide solution in mol dm^{-3}.
(g) Calculate the concentration of the undiluted sodium hydroxide solution in g dm^{-3}.

Answers

(a)

$$\text{moles} = \frac{\text{solution volume (cm}^3) \times \text{concentration (mol dm}^{-3})}{1000} = \frac{17.2 \times 0.02}{1000} = 3.44 \times 10^{-4} \text{ mol}$$

(b) NaOH + HCl → NaCl + H$_2$O
(c) 1:1 ratio of NaOH:HCl so moles of NaOH in 25.0 cm^3 = 3.44 × 10^{-4}
(d) concentration = number of moles in 25.0 cm^3 × 40
= 3.44 × 10^{-4} × 40 = 0.01376 mol dm^{-3}
(e) Dilution factor is × 10 (25 into 250 cm^3) so concentration = 0.01376 × 10
= 0.1376 mol dm^{-3}
(f) concentration in g dm^{-3} = concentration in mol dm^{-3} × RFM
concentration = 0.1376 × 40 (RFM of NaOH) = 5.504 g dm^{-3}

or

(d) number of moles in 250 cm^3 = number of moles in 25 cm^3 × 10 = 3.44 × 10^{-4} × 10
= 3.44 × 10^{-3} mol
(e) This is the same as the number of moles present in 250 cm^3 of the diluted solution
= 3.44 × 10^{-3}
(f) concentration = number of moles in 25.0 cm^3 × 40
= 3.44 × 10^{-3} × 40 = 0.1376 mol dm^{-3}
(g) concentration in g dm^{-3} = concentration in mol dm^{-3} × RFM
concentration = 0.1376 × 40 (RFM of NaOH) = 5.504 g dm^{-3}

This style of acid–base titration question is common and the only differences may be the ratio in the reaction and whether or not there is a dilution.

Degree of hydration titrations

Titrations can also be used to determine the degree of hydration of a salt but the salt in solution must react with an acid so hydrated sodium carbonate is a common example but it could be applied to any hydrated carbonate.

Typical degree of hydration titration

- Dissolve hydrated salt (usually hydrated sodium carbonate) in water and make up the volume to $250\,cm^3$.
- Pipette $25.0\,cm^3$ of sodium carbonate solution into a conical flask.
- Titrate with 0.1 M hydrochloric acid using methyl orange indicator.
- The average titre can be used to calculate moles of hydrochloric acid.

$$Na_2CO_3 + 2HCl \rightarrow 2NaCl + CO_2 + H_2O$$

- Calculate moles of sodium carbonate in $25.0\,cm^3$ of solution using the equation ratio above.
- Calculate moles of sodium carbonate in $250.0\,cm^3$ of solution.
- Use mass and moles in $250.0\,cm^3$ to calculate RFM of $Na_2CO_3.xH_2O$.
- Subtract 106 for Na_2CO_3 — this will give you the RFM of all the water.
- Divide by 18 to calculate moles of water.

Typical degree of hydration calculation question

$2.86\,g$ of hydrated sodium carbonate, $Na_2CO_3.xH_2O$, are dissolved in deionised water, placed in a volumetric flask and the volume made up to $250.0\,cm^3$ using deionised water. A $25.0\,cm^3$ sample of this solution was pipetted into a conical flask and titrated against $0.1\,mol\,dm^{-3}$ hydrochloric acid using methyl orange indicator. The average titre was found to be $20.0\,cm^3$.

Standard types of part questions asked

(a) Calculate the number of moles of hydrochloric acid added from the burette.
(b) Write a balanced symbol equation for the reaction between sodium carbonate and hydrochloric acid.
(c) Calculate the number of moles of sodium carbonate present in $25.0\,cm^3$ of the solution.
(d) Calculate the number of moles of sodium carbonate present in $250.0\,cm^3$ of the solution.

From this point the calculation can go one of two ways.

RFM method

(e) Calculate the RFM of hydrated sodium carbonate using the initial mass and the number of moles.
(f) Calculate the value of x in $Na_2CO_3.xH_2O$.

Ratio method

(e) Calculate the mass of anhydrous sodium carbonate present in the sample.
(f) Calculate the mass of water present in the hydrated sodium carbonate.
(g) Calculate the number of moles of water present in the hydrated salt.
(h) Calculate the value of x in $Na_2CO_3.xH_2O$

Answers

(a)

$$\text{moles} = \frac{\text{solution volume} \times \text{concentration}}{1000} = \frac{20.0 \times 0.1}{1000} = 0.002$$

(b) $Na_2CO_3 + 2HCl \rightarrow 2NaCl + H_2O + CO_2$

(c) 1:2 ratio of Na_2CO_3:HCl so moles of Na_2CO_3 in 25.0 cm^3 = 0.001

(d) moles of Na_2CO_3 present in 250.0 cm^3 = 0.001 × 10 = 0.01

RFM method

(e)

$$\text{RFM} = \frac{\text{mass}}{\text{moles}} = \frac{2.86}{0.01} = 286$$

(f) Na_2CO_3 RFM = 106

RFM of H_2O in $Na_2CO_3.xH_2O$ = 286 − 106 = 180

$$x = \frac{\text{total of RFM of water}}{\text{RFM of water}}$$

$$x = \frac{180}{18} = 10$$

Ratio method

(e) mass = moles × RFM

mass = 0.01 × 106 = 1.06 g

(f) mass of H_2O = 2.86 − 1.06

= 1.8 g

(g)

$$\text{moles of } H_2O = \frac{1.8}{18} = 0.1$$

(h) ratio Na_2CO_3:H_2O = 0.01:0.1

= 1:10   so $x = 10$

Back titration

A back titration is used to determine the purity of a Group II metal, Group II oxide or Group II carbonate. It is used when the substance under analysis is not soluble in water but will react with an acid.

Typical method of back titration

- Solid Group II metal/carbonate/oxide (mass = xg) is added to excess hydrochloric acid (usually 50 cm^3 of 1 M, but can vary).
- 25.0 cm^3 of this solution is pipetted into a 250 cm^3 volumetric flask and diluted to 250.0 cm^3 with deionised water.
- Titrate 25.0 cm^3 of this solution (containing the excess acid) against 0.1 M sodium hydroxide solution using phenolphthalein indicator.
- Colour change: colourless to pink
- Titre = V_1

Typical method of calculation

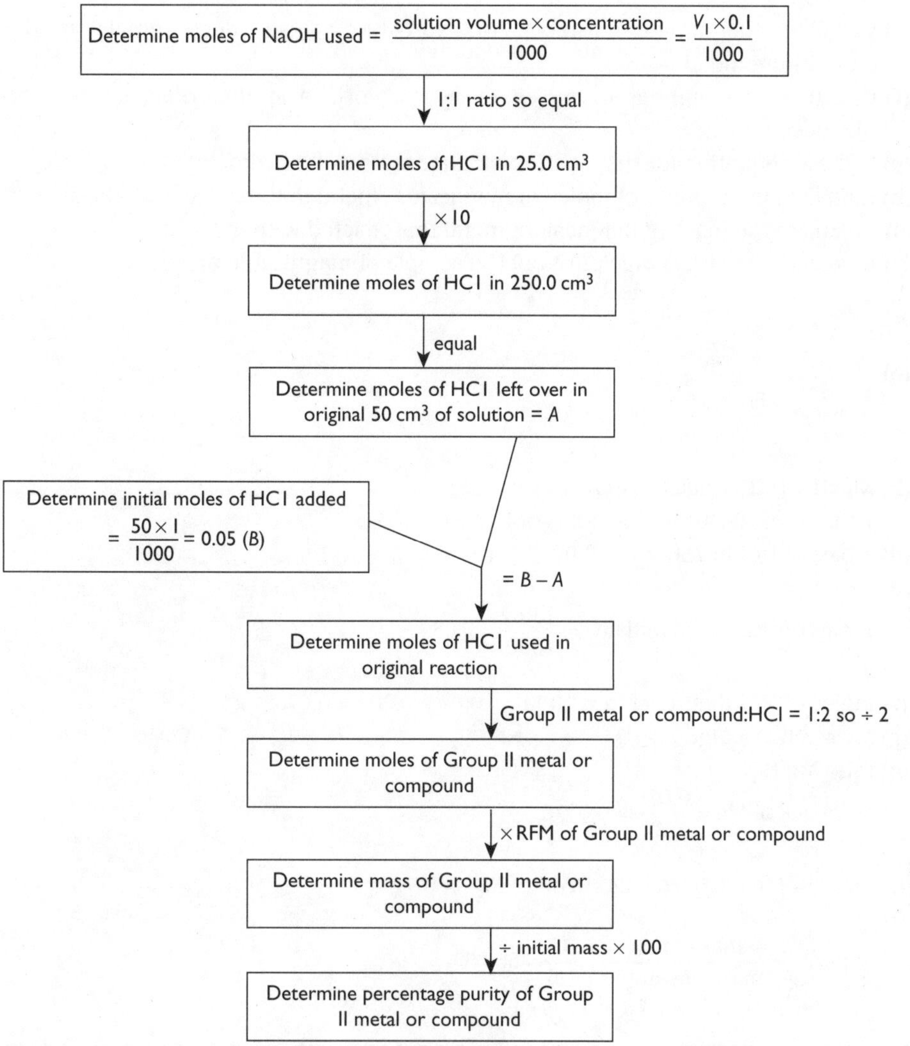

$$\boxed{\text{Determine moles of NaOH used} = \frac{\text{solution volume} \times \text{concentration}}{1000} = \frac{V_1 \times 0.1}{1000}}$$

↓ 1:1 ratio so equal

$$\boxed{\text{Determine moles of HCl in } 25.0 \text{ cm}^3}$$

↓ × 10

$$\boxed{\text{Determine moles of HCl in } 250.0 \text{ cm}^3}$$

↓ equal

$$\boxed{\text{Determine moles of HCl left over in original 50 cm}^3 \text{ of solution} = A}$$

$$\boxed{\text{Determine initial moles of HCl added} = \frac{50 \times 1}{1000} = 0.05 \ (B)}$$

= B − A

$$\boxed{\text{Determine moles of HCl used in original reaction}}$$

↓ Group II metal or compound:HCl = 1:2 so ÷ 2

$$\boxed{\text{Determine moles of Group II metal or compound}}$$

↓ × RFM of Group II metal or compound

$$\boxed{\text{Determine mass of Group II metal or compound}}$$

↓ ÷ initial mass × 100

$$\boxed{\text{Determine percentage purity of Group II metal or compound}}$$

Figure 52

Typical back titration calculation question

1.6 g of a sample of impure magnesium metal were dissolved in 40 cm^3 of 2 mol dm^{-3} hydrochloric acid. The solution was filtered into a 250 cm^3 volumetric flask and the volume made up to 250 cm^3 using deionised water. A 25.0 cm^3 sample of this solution was titrated against 0.02 M sodium hydroxide solution using phenolphthalein indicator. The average titre was determined to be 25.0 cm^3.

Standard types of part questions asked

(a) Calculate the number of moles of sodium hydroxide used.
(b) Write an equation for the reaction of sodium hydroxide with hydrochloric acid.
(c) Calculate the number of moles of hydrochloric acid present in the conical flask.

(d) Calculate the number of moles of hydrochloric acid present in $250\,cm^3$ of the solution.

(e) Calculate the number of moles of hydrochloric acid added initially to the magnesium metal.

(f) Calculate the number of moles of hydrochloric acid that reacted with the magnesium metal.

(g) Write an equation for the reaction of magnesium with hydrochloric acid.

(h) Calculate the number of moles of magnesium metal that reacted with the acid.

(i) Calculate the mass of magnesium metal that reacted with the acid.

(j) Calculate the percentage purity of the sample of magnesium metal.

Answers

(a)

$$moles = \frac{25 \times 0.02}{1000} = 0.0005 \text{ mol}$$

(b) $NaOH + HCl \rightarrow NaCl + H_2O$

(c) 1:1 ratio of NaOH:HCl so moles of HCl = 0.0005

(d) moles of HCl in $250\,cm^3 = 0.0005 \times 10 = 0.005$

(e)

$$moles \text{ of HCl added initially} = \frac{40 \times 2}{1000} = 0.08$$

(f) moles of HCl that reacted with Mg = 0.08 − 0.005 = 0.075

(g) $Mg + 2HCl \rightarrow MgCl_2 + H_2$

(h) ratio Mg:HCl = 1:2

$$\text{so moles of Mg} = \frac{0.075}{2} = 0.0375$$

(i) mass of Mg = 0.0375 × 24 (RAM of Mg) = 0.9 g

(j)

$$\% \text{ purity} = \frac{\text{mass of Mg}}{\text{mass of sample}} = \frac{0.9}{1.6} = 56.25\%$$

Summary

- A titration is carried out using a pipette and burette and two solutions are mixed to determine the exact volume of one solution required to react with an exact volume of the other solution.

- Questions on acid–base titrations are common where one solution is a base (an alkali) and the other is an acid.

- An indicator is used to determine the exact point when the acid has neutralised the base, or vice versa.

- Two common indicators are phenolphthalein and methyl orange.

- The preparation (including rinsings) and accurate use of the apparatus are important in obtaining reliable results.

- The volume of solution added from the burette is called the titre. One rough and two accurate titrations are carried out and the average titre is the average of the two accurate titres.

- Calculations are carried out based on the average titre to determine concentration, number of moles, mass, RFM, percentage purity, degree of hydration and even the identity of unknown elements.

Questions & Answers

The unit test

The AS Unit 1 examination is 1 hour 30 minutes in length and consists of 10 multiple-choice questions (each worth 2 marks) and several structured questions, which vary in length. The structured questions make up the remaining 80 marks, giving 100 marks in total for the paper. For each multiple-choice question there is one correct answer and at least one very clear distractor.

About this section

Each question in this section is followed by brief guidance on how to approach the question and also where you could make errors (shown by the icon ⓔ). Answers to some questions are then followed by examiner's comments. These are preceded by the icon ⓔ. You could try the questions first to see how you get on and then check the answers and comments.

Formulae, equations and amounts of substance

Question 1

Which of the following contains the greatest number of atoms?

A 32 g of sulfur molecules, S_8

B 24 g of magnesium atoms, Mg

C 4 g of hydrogen molecules, H_2

D 31 g of phosphorus molecules, P_4

ⓔ In this question you can easily calculate the number of particles. Calculate the number of moles using the RFM of the formula given and then multiply by N_A to work out the number of atoms for B and the number of molecules for A, C and D. The number of atoms for A, C and D can be determined by multiplying the number of molecules by the number of atoms in each molecule.

A mass (g)/RFM = 32/256 = 0.125 mol $\times N_A$ (6.02 $\times 10^{23}$) = 7.525 $\times 10^{22}$ molecules of S_8
Each S_8 contains 8 sulfur atoms so number of atoms = 8 $\times$ 7.525 $\times 10^{22}$
= 6.02 $\times 10^{23}$ atoms of S

B mass (g)/RFM = 24/24 = 1 mol $\times N_A$ (6.02 $\times 10^{23}$) = 6.02 $\times 10^{23}$ atoms of Mg

C mass (g)/RFM = 4/2 = 2 mol $\times N_A$ (6.02 $\times 10^{23}$) = 1.204 $\times 10^{24}$ molecules of H_2
Each H_2 contains 2 hydrogen atoms so number of atoms = 2 $\times$ 1.204 $\times 10^{24}$
= 2.408 $\times 10^{24}$ atoms of H

D mass (g)/RFM = 31/124 = 0.25 mol $\times N_A$ (6.02 $\times 10^{23}$) = 1.505 $\times 10^{23}$ molecules of P_4
Each P_4 contains 4 phosphorus atoms so number of atoms = 4 $\times$ 1.505 $\times 10^{23}$
= 6.02 $\times 10^{23}$ atoms of P

Answer is C

Question 2

Phosphorus, P_4, reacts with bromine to form the colourless liquid phosphorus tribromide, PBr_3.

(a) Write an equation for the reaction of phosphorus, P_4, with bromine to form phosphorus tribromide. (1 mark)

ⓔ When you are given P_4 in the question you will be expected to use it in the equation. The most common mistake would be to use P instead of P_4. As the question is only worth 1 mark any mistake will lose the mark.

(a) $P_4 + 6Br_2 \rightarrow 4PBr_3$

(b) **Using the following headings, calculate the mass of phosphorus tribromide formed if 3.1 g of phosphorus is reacted with 10 cm³ of bromine (density of liquid bromine is 3.1 g cm⁻³).**
- **mass of bromine, Br_2, in grams** (1 mark)
- **moles of bromine, Br_2** (1 mark)
- **moles of phosphorus, P_4, in 3.1 g** (1 mark)
- **limiting reactant** (1 mark)
- **moles of phosphorus tribromide formed** (1 mark)
- **mass of phosphorus tribromide formed** (1 mark)

ⓔ The headings make this question more approachable as you know how each mark is awarded. Work through it as far as you can. Each step you get right will get you a mark, plus marks in calculations are carried through so if you think you have made a mistake, going on with the rest of the question using the correct process but with the wrong numbers will still be credited.

Always scan through the whole question to see where it is leading. In this case 'limiting reactant' and 'density of liquid bromine is 3.1 g cm⁻³' give you clues as to what type of calculation is expected. If you get a bit lost, try to finish the question with any values you have or simply pick a reactant for limiting and finish the question using this one.

(b) mass of bromine = volume × density = 10 × 3.1 = 31 g ✓

moles of bromine, Br_2 = 31/160 = 0.194 mol ✓

moles of P_4 = 3.1/124 = 0.025 ✓

limiting reactant: based on equation $P_4 + 6Br_2 \rightarrow 4PBr_3$

0.025 mol of P_4 react with 0.150 mol of Br_2 *but* 0.194 mol of Br_2 is present so Br_2 is in excess.

P_4 is the limiting reactant. ✓

Based on moles of P_4 (limiting reactant), moles of PBr_3 formed = 0.025 × 4 = 0.1 mol ✓

mass of PBr_3 formed = mass × RFM = 0.1 × 271 = 27.1 g ✓

Question 3

4.75 g of a hydrated sample of copper(II) sulfate, $CuSO_4.xH_2O$ were heated to constant mass. The mass reduced by 1.71 g. Which of the following is the value of x?

A 3

B 4

C 5

D 6

ⓔ The masses that need to be determined in this style of calculation are the mass of the anhydrous copper(II) sulfate and the mass of water lost. Read the question carefully. The decrease in mass on heating to constant mass is the mass of water lost (= 1.71 g). The mass of the anhydrous solid, $CuSO_4$, is the mass remaining after heating to constant mass (= 4.75 − 1.71 = 3.04 g). The moles of anhydrous solid and water can be determined and the simplest ratio worked out.

moles of anhydrous solid, $CuSO_4$ = 3.04/160 = 0.019 mol

moles of water = 1.71/18 = 0.095 mol

simplest ratio of $CuSO_4:H_2O$ = 1:5 so x = 5

Answer is C

Atomic structure

Question 1

Approximately how many electrons would have the same mass as the mass of one neutron?

A 20

B 200

C 2000

D 20 000

ⓔ This question relies on the fact that you know that one electron has a relative mass of 1/1840 of that of a proton and a neutron. This means that 1840 electrons would have the mass of one neutron.

Answer is C

Question 2

Which of the following is the electronic configuration of a titanium ion, Ti^{2+}?

A $1s^2\,2s^2\,2p^6\,3s^2\,3p^6\,4s^2$

B $1s^2\,2s^2\,2p^6\,3s^2\,3p^6\,3d^2\,4s^2$

C $1s^2\,2s^2\,2p^6\,3s^2\,3p^6\,3d^4$

D $1s^2\,2s^2\,2p^6\,3s^2\,3p^6\,3d^2$

ⓔ The atomic number of titanium is 22 so a titanium atom has 22 protons and 22 electrons. The Ti^{2+} ion has lost two electrons and remember that transition metal atoms lose 4s electrons first. The electronic configuration of a titanium ion, Ti^{2+}, is $1s^2\, 2s^2\, 2p^6\, 3s^2\, 3p^6\, 3d^2$ — the $4s^2$ electrons were lost.

Answer is D

Question 3

(a) **Write an equation for the first ionisation energy of potassium, including state symbols.** (2 marks)

(a) $K(g) \rightarrow K^+(g) + e^-$ ✓ ✓

ⓔ 1 mark is awarded for the correct equation and 1 mark for the correct state symbols. To answer this, remember the definition of first ionisation energy — the key points are gaseous atoms losing one mole of electrons and forming gaseous monopositive ions. The most common error in this answer would be incorrect state symbols for the potassium atom and the ion. Some answers might attempt to include a state symbol for the electron. Electrons are lost so should appear on the right-hand side of the equation.

(b) **Explain why the first ionisation energy of rubidium is smaller than the first ionisation energy of potassium.** (2 marks)

(b) Outer electron for rubidium further from the nucleus/atomic radius increases. ✓
Outer electron is shielded by more inner shells of electrons. ✓

ⓔ The main point in any question on differences in ionisation energies is to identify which of the four factors that affect ionisation energies apply to this answer. They are atomic radius, (effective) nuclear charge, shielding by inner electrons and stability of filled and half-filled subshells. Both potassium and rubidium have outer-shell s^1 electronic configurations so there is no difference in stability of filled or half-filled subshells. The (effective) nuclear charge is the same as both atoms have equal numbers of protons and electrons, so net attraction is the same. For rubidium it is the increasing atomic radius (distance from the nucleus) and more shielding by inner electrons that causes the decrease in first ionisation energy.

Question 4

Which one of the following electron transitions is responsible for the lowest frequency line in the ultraviolet region of the emission spectrum of atomic hydrogen?

A $n = 1$ to $n = 2$

B $n = 2$ to $n = 1$

C $n = 2$ to $n = 3$

D $n = 3$ to $n = 2$

ⓔ In this question there are three key parts that lead you to the answer: *lowest frequency line*, *ultraviolet region* and *emission spectrum*. The ultraviolet region must involve $n = 1$; the lowest transition to and from $n = 1$ is from $n = 2$ and emission indicates that the electrons are falling to lower energy levels, so the transition must be from $n = 2$ to $n = 1$. This type of question is common as a multiple-choice question (worth 2 marks) or as a structured question in which you may be expected to label the energy levels and draw an arrow from one energy level to another to represent the electron transition. The structured question is usually worth 3 marks — 1 mark for the correct starting energy level, 1 mark for the correct end energy level and 1 mark for the correct direction of the arrow.

Answer is B

Question 5

The mass spectrum of zirconium (atomic number 40) indicates five different isotopes, which have the following relative abundances.

Relative isotopic mass	Relative abundance
90	51.5
91	11.2
92	17.1
94	17.4
96	2.8

Calculate the relative atomic mass of zirconium to two decimal places. (3 marks)

ⓔ When calculating relative atomic mass from relative isotopic masses data or from a mass spectrum directly, you should multiply the mass by the relative abundance for each isotope, then add them all up. Finally divide by the total of all the relative abundances. If the question asks for a specific number of decimal places, stick to this or you will lose a mark.

$$\text{relative atomic mass} = \frac{(90 \times 51.5) + (91 \times 11.2) + (92 \times 17.1) + (94 \times 17.4) + (96 \times 2.8)}{51.5 + 11.2 + 17.1 + 17.4 + 2.8} \checkmark$$

$$= \frac{9131.8}{100}$$

$$= 91.318 \checkmark = 91.32 \checkmark \text{ to 2 decimal places}$$

Bonding

Question 1

Chlorine reacts with magnesium to form magnesium chloride. Magnesium chloride is soluble in water and magnesium chloride solution conducts electricity.

(a) Using a dot-and-cross diagram, explain how atoms of magnesium react with atoms of chlorine to form magnesium chloride. Show outer electrons only.

(4 marks)

(a)

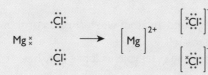

🄔 Magnesium chloride is an ionic compound. Only show outer electrons in the answer. Magnesium atoms have 2 outer electrons and chlorine atoms have 7 outer electrons.

1 magnesium atom requires 2 chlorine atoms. Draw all the atoms showing a cross (×) for electrons on one type of atom and a dot (•) for the electrons on the other type of atom. Each of the 2 outer electrons of the magnesium atom transfers to each chlorine atom (still draw as an × to show where they came from). The magnesium ion now has no electrons in this outer shell and each chloride ion has 8 electrons in its outer shell. Show the charges on the ions.
- Correct electronic configuration of Mg atom ✓
- Correct electronic configuration of Cl atom ✓
- Correct number of each atom/ion, i.e. 1:2 ratio ✓
- Correct electron transfer and charges on the ions ✓

(b) Explain why a solution of magnesium chloride conducts electricity.

(2 marks)

(b) Magnesium chloride is an ionic compound and when dissolved in water the ions ✓ are free to move and carry charge ✓.

ⓔ The most common error here is to confuse ions and electrons. Metals and graphite conduct electricity due to the delocalised electrons, which are free to move and carry charge, but molten ionic compounds, ionic compounds dissolved in water and acids all conduct electricity due to the free ions that can move and carry charge. You will lose a mark if you confuse the charged particles that can move.

Question 2

Beryllium chloride is a covalently bonded molecule, as shown in the dot-and-cross diagram.

:C̈l: Be :C̈l:

(a) Explain why beryllium chloride does not obey the octet rule. (2 marks)

ⓔ The octet rule states that when forming a compound an atom will lose, gain or share electrons to achieve 8 electrons in its outer shell. You must state the octet rule and then explain which atom(s) obey or do not obey it and how they do not obey it. In this example it is the beryllium atom that does not obey the octet rule but you must explain clearly how (Be has only 4 electrons in its outer shell).

(a) When forming a compound an atom will lose, gain or share electrons to achieve 8 electrons in its outer shell. ✓
Be atom does not obey the octet rule as it has only has 4 electrons in its outer shell. ✓

(b) Explain the term electronegativity. (2 marks)

ⓔ This is a common definition style question and it is important that you include all aspects of the definition to gain the marks. Do not change it, and make sure you use the proper scientific terms as often one wrong word can cost you a mark.

(b) A numerical value that indicates the extent to which an atom in a covalent bond ✓ will attract the bonding electrons ✓.

(c) Label the diagram below to show the polarity of the Be–Cl bond. (1 mark)
Be—Cl

ⓔ This question is essentially asking about the trends in electronegativity of elements. The more electronegative atom will be $\delta-$ and the other $\delta+$. Atoms that are further to the right in the Periodic Table are more electronegative and those further up the Periodic Table are more electronegative. Cl is much further to the right and so is more electronegative, so Cl gets the $\delta-$ and Be the $\delta+$. Make sure you write them above the atoms to indicate the polarity.

(c) $\delta+$ $\delta-$
        Be—Cl

(d) Explain why beryllium chloride is a non-polar molecular even though it contains polar bonds.   (2 marks)

🄴 This is a common question as many molecules are non-polar even though they contain polar bonds. The molecules like this must contain equally polar bonds, which are arranged symmetrically so the polarities (dipoles) of these bonds cancel each other out. Common examples are CO_2, CCl_4 and BF_3. Similar molecules like CS_2, CF_4 and BCl_3 would also be non-polar for the same reasons.

(d) Beryllium chloride contains equally polar bonds which are arranged symmetrically ✓ and so the polarities of the bonds (dipoles) cancel each other out ✓.

Question 4

Which of the following does not have a molecular covalent crystalline structure?

A diamond

B ice

C iodine

D rhombic sulfur

🄴 This question can be approached in two ways as it is a negative question. Highlight the *not* to remind you. Describe the structure of each and decide which one does not exist as molecular covalent crystals. All are crystalline solids but diamond is giant covalent; the rest are molecular covalent.

Answer is A

Shapes of molecules

Question 1

Which of the following gives the correct shapes of the molecules ammonia, water and carbon dioxide?

	Ammonia shape	Water shape	Carbon dioxide shape
A	Tetrahedral	Linear	Bent
B	Pyramidal	Linear	Linear
C	Trigonal planar	Bent	Linear
D	Pyramidal	Bent	Linear

ⓔ It is important to remember the shapes of various molecules. Water is often wrongly identified as linear and ammonia as trigonal planar. Carbon dioxide is linear due to the equal repulsion of the bonding electrons in the double bonds. Remember that molecules with two bonds can be linear or bent; molecules with three bonds can be trigonal planar or pyramidal.

Answer is D

Question 2

The diagram below is a dot-and-cross diagram for phosphine, PH_3.

$$\overset{\times\times}{H \overset{\cdot}{\underset{\cdot\times}{P}} \times H}$$
$$H$$

State and explain the shape of a molecule of phosphine. (4 marks)

ⓔ It is common to base such a question on a familiar compound but change the central atom to that of another element in the same group. PH_3 is similar to NH_3. The explanation of its shape is the same as the explanation for NH_3. This can also be done with H_2S (similar to H_2O), SiH_4 (similar to CH_4) etc.

- shape of PH_3 pyramidal ✓
- electron pairs repel each other ✓
- three bonding pairs of electrons and one lone pair of electrons and lone pair has a greater repulsion ✓
- takes up shape to minimise repulsions ✓

Intermolecular forces

Question I

> **Which of the following liquids is polar?**
>
> **A** CCl_4
>
> **B** CS_2
>
> **C** C_2H_5OH
>
> **D** C_6H_{14}

ⓔ This type of question can be asked in many different ways and the molecules chosen can vary. Again, use your knowledge of shape and polarity to decide which are the non-polar molecules. CS_2 will be non-polar based on CO_2 being non-polar. All hydrocarbons are non-polar. CCl_4 and CS_2 both contain polar bonds but the bonds are arranged symmetrically so the polarities cancel out, making the molecules non-polar overall. The question could ask 'a stream of which liquid would be deflected by a charged rod'. A stream of polar liquid would be deflected by a charged rod.

> Answer is C

Question 2

> **Iodine is a molecular covalent crystalline solid that has van der Waals forces of attraction. Van der Waals forces are a type of intermolecular bonding.**
>
> **(a) State one other type of intermolecular bonding.** (1 mark)
>
> **(b) Explain how van der Waals forces of attraction arise between molecules.** (2 marks)

ⓔ There are three types of intermolecular forces between simple covalent molecules: van der Waals forces of attraction, permanent dipole attractions and hydrogen bonds. You need to be able to recognise which forces of attraction occur between specific molecules. Remember that non-polar molecules (such as I_2) only have van der Waals forces of attraction between their molecules. Polar molecules will have permanent dipole attractions and if a polar molecule has a hydrogen atom bonded to a N, O or F atom, this H atom can form a hydrogen bond with any electronegative atom with a lone pair of electrons. Make sure that you can explain how the intermolecular forces are formed.

> **(a)** hydrogen bonds/permanent dipole attractions ✓
> **(b)** temporary dipoles ✓ caused by random movement of electrons ✓

Question 3

Explain why water has a higher boiling point than hydrogen sulfide. (3 marks)

ⓔ Any question about physical state or melting/boiling points of simple covalent substances is linked to intermolecular forces. It is vital that you can correctly identify a substance as simple covalent and then identify the intermolecular forces that are needed to explain the properties. Water forms stronger hydrogen bonds between its molecules as well as van der Waals forces of attraction whereas hydrogen sulfide, H_2S, has weaker van der Waals forces of attraction and permanent dipole attractions. The answer must give the type of intermolecular bonding and say which is stronger. Give a full answer, bringing in the idea of the energy required to break the bonds to ensure you gain all the marks.

Hydrogen bonds between water molecules ✓ are stronger than van der Waals forces of attraction/permanent dipole attraction in H_2S ✓.

More energy is needed to break the stronger hydrogen bonds. ✓

Redox

Question 1

Explain, in terms of oxidation numbers, why the following reaction is described as a redox reaction. (3 marks)

$6FeSO_4 + 3Cl_2 \rightarrow 2Fe_2(SO_4)_3 + 2FeCl_3$

Iron/Fe is oxidised from +2 (in $FeSO_4$) to +3 (in $Fe_2(SO_4)_3$) and in $FeCl_3$. ✓

Chlorine is reduced from 0 (in Cl_2) to –1 (in $FeCl_3$). ✓

Redox is oxidation and reduction occurring in the same reaction. ✓

ⓔ Most answers will achieve the final mark but many will confuse the calculation of the oxidation numbers. Remember that the sulfate ion is SO_4^{2-} so the iron (Fe) in $FeSO_4$ has an oxidation number of +2 and the iron (Fe) in both $Fe_2(SO_4)_3$ and $FeCl_3$ has an oxidation number of +3. All compounds have an overall oxidation number of 0. All elements, even diatomic ones like chlorine, Cl_2, have an oxidation number of 0. The balancing numbers in the equation do not affect the oxidation number. The sulfate ion, SO_4^{2-} does not change so the oxidation number of the sulfur or oxygen also does not change.

Question 2

For the following half-equation, *a*, *b* and *c* are the number of moles of water, hydrogen ions and electrons required respectively.

$$SO_2 + aH_2O \rightarrow SO_4^{2-} + bH^+ + ce^-$$

Which one of the following is correct?

	a	*b*	*c*
A	1	2	2
B	2	2	2
C	2	2	4
D	2	4	2

ⓔ To answer this question, calculate the oxidation number of sulfur in SO_2 (+4) and in SO_4^{2-} (+6). The equation is an oxidation as the electrons are being lost (on the right-hand side of the equation), so there must be an increase in oxidation number. Two moles of water are required on the left to supply the extra oxygen atoms and $4H^+$ must be a product. Practise balancing these equations but watch out for the dichromate(VI) one, where the ratio of dichromate to Cr^{3+} is 1:2.

Answer is D

Question 3

Using the half-equations shown below:

$$MnO_4^- + 8H^+ + 5e^- \rightarrow Mn^{2+} + 4H_2O$$

$$2Br^- \rightarrow Br_2 + 2e^-$$

Write an ionic equation for the oxidation of bromide ions using acidified potassium manganate(VII). (2 marks)

ⓔ Before tackling this question it is important to remember that an ionic equation does not contain electrons. You must combine an oxidation and reduction half-equation, multiplying each if necessary so that the electrons cancel out on each side. Remember for more complex ionic equations you may have to cancel down H^+ ions and H_2O as well to simplify the final equation. In this example multiply the manganate(VII) half-equation by 2 and multiply the bromide half-equation by 5. Then add the equations together by writing down everything on the left of both arrows then putting an arrow before writing down everything on the right of the arrows. Then cancel out anything that appears on both sides (in this case $10e^-$) and you have the finished ionic equation.

$$2MnO_4^- + 16H^+ + 10e^- \rightarrow 2Mn^{2+} + 8H_2O$$

$$10Br^- \rightarrow 5Br_2 + 10e^-$$

$$2MnO_4^- + 16H^+ + 10e^- + 10Br^- \rightarrow 2Mn^{2+} + 8H_2O + 5Br_2 + 10e^-$$

Ionic equation:

$$2MnO_4^- + 16H^+ + 10Br^- \rightarrow 2Mn^{2+} + 8H_2O + 5Br_2 \; ✓ ✓$$

The Periodic Table and Group VII

Question 1

Which one of the following lists increasing acid strength of 1 M solutions of the hydrogen halides?

A	HF	HCl	HBr	HI
B	HCl	HI	HBr	HF
C	HI	HBr	HF	HCl
D	HI	HBr	HCl	HF

(e) The covalent bond enthalpy of the hydrogen halides decreases with increasing bond length. Hydrogen iodide has the longest (and weakest) covalent bond of the hydrogen halides as the iodine atom is the largest of these halogen atoms. In solution the HI hydrolyses most, producing a higher concentration of H^+ ions and so a greater acid strength. HBr is next, then HCl and finally the weakest acid strength is for HF.

> Answer is A

Question 2

Sodium iodide reacts with concentrated sulfuric acid.

(a) Name all the products of the reaction. (3 marks)

(b) State what you would observe during the reaction. (3 marks)

(c) Write two balanced symbol equations for the reactions that are occurring. (2 marks)

(e) Remember that the equations for the reactions of the halides with concentrated sulfuric acid are very similar, with the first equation being common to the chloride, bromide and iodide; the second is common to the bromide and iodide. The last two equations must be recalled for the iodide, but knowing the equations allows you to name all the products as well as stating observations for the reactions. So it is best to answer part (c) first and use the equations to answer parts (a) and (b). If the equations are not asked for, write them down to remind yourself. You will not lose marks for incorrect equations if they are not asked for.

(c) $NaI + H_2SO_4 \rightarrow HI + NaHSO_4$
$2HI + H_2SO_4 \rightarrow I_2 + SO_2 + 2H_2O$
$6HI + H_2SO_4 \rightarrow 3I_2 + S + 4H_2O$
$8HI + H_2SO_4 \rightarrow 4I_2 + H_2S + 4H_2O$

🅔 Any two score 1 mark each.

(a) hydrogen iodide; sodium hydrogen sulfate; iodine; sulfur dioxide; water; sulfur; hydrogen sulfide ✓ ✓ ✓

🅔 For all seven products named correctly 3 marks are awarded. Six products named correctly gain 2 marks. Five products named correctly gain 1 mark. Four or fewer products named correctly gain no marks.

(b) *Any three from*:
- misty/steamy fumes
- pungent gas
- purple vapour/grey-black solid
- yellow solid
- rotten eggs smell
- heat released ✓ ✓ ✓

Question 3

A solid compound was dissolved in deionised water. Dilute nitric acid was added followed by silver nitrate solution. A white precipitate was observed, which dissolved when ammonia solution was added.

(a) Name the ion that has been identified during this test. (1 mark)

(b) Write an ionic equation for the formation of the white precipitate. (1 mark)

(c) Explain why dilute nitric acid is added to the solution before silver nitrate solution. (2 marks)

🅔 Silver nitrate solution is the key to this question as it is used to test for halide (chloride, bromide and iodide) ions. The dilute nitric acid is added to remove any carbonate ions, which would give a white precipitate of silver carbonate, Ag_2CO_3. This would be a false positive test for chloride ions. Learn the observations carefully in terms of the colour of the precipitates and whether they redissolve in ammonia solution.

(a) chloride ✓
(b) $Ag^+ + Cl^- \rightarrow AgCl$ ✓
(c) Nitric acid reacts with/removes carbonate ions. ✓
Carbonate ions would give a white precipitate/false test for chloride ions. ✓

Question 4

State the colour of each of the following:

(a) NaBr(s)   (1 mark)

(b) Cl₂(g)   (1 mark)

(c) KI(aq)   (1 mark)

(d) I₂ (dissolved in hexane)   (1 mark)

(a) white ✓
(b) yellow-green ✓
(c) colourless ✓
(d) purple ✓

ⓔ Questions concerning the colours of the halogens and halides are common and you should learn these thoroughly. Remember that Group I and II halides are white solids, which dissolve in water forming colourless solutions. Most of these questions are recall (AO1) and these are marks you cannot afford to lose. Often they may be asked as observations for reactions, but knowing the colours can help you deduce what should be observed.

Question 5

Which of the following shows the general trends in atomic radius across a period and down a group in the Periodic Table?

	Trend across a period	Trend down a group
A	Decreases	Decreases
B	Decreases	Increases
C	Increases	Decreases
D	Increases	Increases

ⓔ Across a period atomic radius decreases and down a group atomic radius increases. This question could be applied to any trend such as electronegativity, first ionisation energy or melting points. Make sure you know these trends and can apply them as the question might be about two particular elements or a few elements and you need to use your knowledge of the trends in an unfamiliar context.

Answer is B

Titrations

Question 1

Which one of the following shows the most suitable indicator for the titration?

	Titration	Indicator
A	Ethanoic acid and sodium hydroxide solution	Methyl orange
B	Nitric acid and ammonia solution	Phenolphthalein
C	Sodium hydroxide solution and sulfuric acid	Phenolphthalein
D	Ammonia solution and ethanoic acid	Methyl orange

ⓔ The choice of indicator in a titration depends on the acid and alkali involved. Strong acids (hydrochloric acid, sulfuric acid and nitric acid) reacting with a strong alkali (sodium hydroxide solution or potassium hydroxide solution) can use either phenolphthalein or methyl orange. A strong acid with a weak alkali (mainly ammonia solution or sodium carbonate solution) must use methyl orange. A weak acid (mostly organic acids like ethanoic acid) with a strong alkali must use phenolphthalein and finally for a weak acid with a weak alkali there is no suitable indicator and a pH meter is the most suitable way of monitoring such a titration.

Answer is C

Question 2

20.0 cm³ of 0.03 M sulfuric acid is exactly neutralised by:

A 15.0 cm³ of 0.02 M sodium hydroxide solution

B 15.0 cm³ of 0.04 M sodium hydroxide solution

C 30.0 cm³ of 0.02 M sodium hydroxide solution

D 30.0 cm³ of 0.04 M sodium hydroxide solution

ⓔ The most common error in this question would be to assume a 1:1 ratio in the reaction between sodium hydroxide and sulfuric acid. Always write the balanced symbol equation for the titration reaction to check the ratio:

$$2NaOH + H_2SO_4 \rightarrow Na_2SO_4 + 2H_2O$$

The ratio of NaOH to H_2SO_4 is 2:1. 20.0 cm³ of 0.03 M sulfuric acid is 0.0006 mol. This reacts with 0.0012 mol of NaOH. Which of the answers A to D gives 0.0012 mol of NaOH?

Answer is D

Question 3

0.715 g of a sample of hydrated sodium carbonate, $Na_2CO_3.xH_2O$, were dissolved in deionised water and the volume of the solution was made up to 250 cm^3 in a volumetric flask.

25.0 cm^3 of this sample were titrated against 0.05 mol dm^{-3} hydrochloric acid using methyl orange indicator. The average titre was 12.3 cm^3.

(a) State the colour change observed at the end point. (2 marks)

(b) Calculate the number of moles of hydrochloric acid used in this titration. (1 mark)

(c) Write the equation for the reaction between sodium carbonate and hydrochloric acid. (2 marks)

(d) Calculate the number of moles of sodium carbonate present in 25.0 cm^3 of solution. (1 mark)

(e) Calculate the number of moles of sodium carbonate present in 250 cm^3 of solution. (1 mark)

(f) Calculate the mass of sodium carbonate, Na_2CO_3, present in the sample. (1 mark)

(g) Calculate the mass of water present in the sample of hydrated sodium carbonate. . (1 mark)

(h) Calculate the number of moles of water present in the sample. (1 mark)

(i) Calculate the value of x in $Na_2CO_3.xH_2O$. (1 mark)

e This is a standard type of structured titration question. The question leads you through the answer and guides you to determine the moles of the anhydrous salt and the moles of water and then determine the value of x (degree of hydration) by determining the simplest ratio of anhydrous salt to water.

It is often useful to do a sketch of the titration to make sure you know what is happening at each stage. This can help you work out the colour change of the indicator and also carry out the calculation. For example:

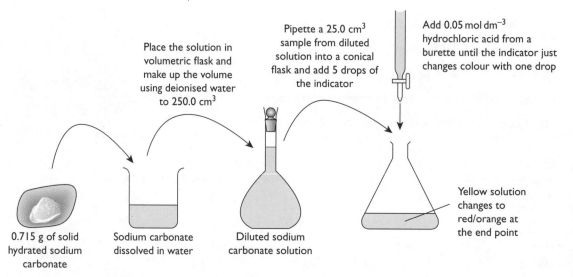

Place the solution in volumetric flask and make up the volume using deionised water to 250.0 cm^3

Pipette a 25.0 cm^3 sample from diluted solution into a conical flask and add 5 drops of the indicator

Add 0.05 mol dm^{-3} hydrochloric acid from a burette until the indicator just changes colour with one drop

0.715 g of solid hydrated sodium carbonate

Sodium carbonate dissolved in water

Diluted sodium carbonate solution

Yellow solution changes to red/orange at the end point

Remember when determining the colour change at the end point that the acid is added to the alkali. This is clear as the average titre is for hydrochloric acid and the average titre is for the solution added from the burette.

(a) yellow ✓ to red/orange ✓

ⓔ Even if you cannot work out which solution is being added from the burette, make an educated guess at the colour change for methyl orange as even the wrong way round will gain 1 mark if 2 marks are on offer.

(b) moles of HCl $= \dfrac{\text{solution volume (cm}^3) \times \text{concentration (mol dm}^{-3})}{1000}$

$= \dfrac{12.3 \times 0.05}{1000}$

$= 0.000615$ ✓ mol

ⓔ The first step in most titration questions is to calculate the number of moles of the solute in the solution added from the burette. Make sure you do not confuse the solution volumes as $25.0\,\text{cm}^3$ was added to the conical flask and $12.3\,\text{cm}^3$ was added from the burette. Check twice that it is the correct solution.

(c) $Na_2CO_3 + 2HCl \rightarrow 2NaCl + CO_2 + H_2O$ ✓ ✓

ⓔ The most common mistake in this equation is to miss the 1:2 ratio of Na_2CO_3:HCl. Practise writing these equations where carbonates of Group I react with strong acids.

(d) 1:2 ratio of Na_2CO_3:HCl so the moles of $Na_2CO_3 = \dfrac{\text{moles of HCl}}{2}$

$= \dfrac{0.000615}{2} = 0.0003075$ ✓

ⓔ The second step in a titration calculation is usually working out the number of moles of solute dissolved in the solution volume (usually $25.0\,\text{cm}^3$) that was pipetted into the conical flask. The ratio of the reaction between the two solutes allows you to do this. 1 mol of Na_2CO_3 reacts with 2 mol of HCl so to move from HCl to Na_2CO_3 you need to divide the number of moles by 2. Think this step out logically each time as errors are often made here with students multiplying by 2 instead of dividing by 2.

(e) $0.0003075 \times 10 = 0.003075$ ✓

ⓔ The number of moles of this solute (Na_2CO_3) in $25.0\,\text{cm}^3$ of solution is multiplied by 10 to determine the number of moles of the solute in $250\,\text{cm}^3$ of the solution as a $25.0\,\text{cm}^3$ sample of the solution was taken, so 1/10th of the moles was taken from the volumetric flask. This is the number of moles of Na_2CO_3 in solution and is the same as the number of moles of solid $Na_2CO_3.xH_2O$ added to the solution. It is important to realise the distinction between solid

$Na_2CO_3.xH_2O$, which is hydrated, and sodium carbonate in solution, which is simply $Na_2CO_3(aq)$. The water of crystallisation is not part of the mass of the solute in solution but the number of moles of each is the same.

(f) $0.003075 \times 106 = 0.326$ ✓ g

ⓔ The mass of Na_2CO_3 dissolved refers to the mass of Na_2CO_3 (not $Na_2CO_3.xH_2O$). You do not know the degree of hydration so you cannot work out an RFM of $Na_2CO_3.xH_2O$. As with all moles–mass calculations, multiply the number of moles by the RFM (in this case 106 for Na_2CO_3).

(g) $0.715 - 0.326 = 0.389$ ✓ g

ⓔ 0.715 g of solid $Na_2CO_3.xH_2O$ was added but only 0.3260 g was determined to be Na_2CO_3. The rest of the mass must be the xH_2O. Subtraction gives the mass of water in $Na_2CO_3.xH_2O$.

(h) $\dfrac{0.389}{18} = 0.0216$ ✓

ⓔ As with all mass–moles calculations, divide the mass by the RFM. The RFM of water is 18 in all calculations.

(i) ratio of $Na_2CO_3:H_2O = 0.003075:0.0216 = 1:7.02 = 1:7$ so $x = 7$

ⓔ Using the moles of Na_2CO_3 determined in part (e) and the moles of water determined in part (h) divided by the smallest number of moles (0.003075) to reduce the ratio to $1:x$, the value of x is determined to be 7.02. Rounding errors during the calculation and also during the titration may have resulted in a rough answer so the answer provided should be the nearest whole number, so $x = 7$. Note that x does not have to be a whole number as hydrated salts lose water of crystallisation gradually over time, so the actual value may be between 6 and 7, but this would be indicated in the question.

Question 4

Describe, giving practical details, how you would accurately prepare a 250 cm³ solution
containing 0.715 g of hydrated sodium carbonate.   (4 marks)

- Weigh accurately 0.715 g of hydrated sodium carbonate in a container. ✓
- Add (a minimum quantity of) deionised water and stir with a glass rod until
  dissolved. ✓
- Add the solution to a 250 cm³ volumetric flask using a filter funnel. ✓
- Rinse the rod and container (and funnel) into a 250 cm³ volumetric flask through a
  filter funnel, ensuring all rinsings enter the flask. ✓
- Add deionised water until the bottom of the meniscus is on the line. ✓
- Mix the solution by stoppering the flask and inverting it several times. ✓ (*maximum
  4 marks*)

e This type of question is common in AS and A2 practical exams as well as in AS Unit 1 papers.
Make sure you include all the rinsings to make up the solution as well as the idea of the bottom of
the meniscus being on the line in the volumetric flask. Practical detail is key here.

1 6.02×10^{23}
2 52.17
3 $C_3H_2NO_2$
4 1.08g
5 proton: relative mass = 1; relative charge = +1
electron: relative mass = 1/1840; relative charge = −1
neutron: relative mass = 1; relative charge = 0
6 The molecular ion is the ion formed by the removal of one electron from a molecule.
7 The outer shell electrons are in the s subshell.
8 Electrons are promoted to higher energy levels. They fall back to lower energy levels, releasing energy as light.
9 atomic radius; nuclear charge; shielding by inner electrons; stability of filled and half-filled subshells
10 ionic
11 Attraction between positive ions in the lattice and delocalised electrons.
12 A shared pair of electrons.
13 Carbon in methane obeys the octet rule as there are eight electrons in its outer shell
14 Chlorine is more electronegative as it is higher in Group VII.

15 Electron pairs repel each other. The four bonding pairs of electrons repel equally. The molecule takes up a shape to minimise repulsions, in this case tetrahedral.
16 pyramidal; 107°
17 hydrogen bonds; permanent dipoles; van der Waals forces (any two)
18 Fixed hydrogen bonds lead to a more open structure in ice, so a lower density.
19 +5
20 $SO_3^{2-} + 6H^+ + 4e^- \rightarrow S + 3H_2O$
21 The same element is oxidised and reduced in the same reaction.
22 p block; its outer shell electrons are in the p subshell.
23 Ionisation energy increases as nuclear charge increases and atomic radius decreases, so more energy is required to remove the electron.
24 Iodine is a grey-black solid; when heated it is a purple vapour/gas.
25 yellow precipitate
26 $KBr + H_2SO_4 \rightarrow KHSO_4 + HBr$
$2HBr + H_2SO_4 \rightarrow Br_2 + SO_2 + 2H_2O$
27 nitric acid/hydrochloric acid/sulfuric acid (any two)
28 pink to colourless

Note: **bold** page numbers point to definitions of key terms.